AN EXCHANGE OF GIFTS

An Exchange of Gifts

of Gifts

A Storyteller's Handbook

MARION V. RALSTON

Pippin Publishing Limited

Copyright © 1993 by Pippin Publishing Limited
380 Esna Park Drive
Markham
Ontario L3R 1H5

Designed by John Zehethofer
Edited by Helen Mason
Typeset by Jay Tee Graphics Ltd.
Printed and bound in Canada by Hignell Printing Limited

Canadian Cataloguing in Publication Data

Ralston, Marion V. (Marion Virginia), 1932-
    An exchange of gifts

(The Pippin teacher's library ; 6)
Includes bibliographical references.
ISBN 0-88751-040-X

1. Storytelling. I. Title. II. Series.

LB1042.R35 1992   372.6'42   C92-093893-0

10 9 8 7 6 5 4 3 2 1

CONTENTS

. . . .

INTRODUCTION

Storytelling is an exchange of gifts. It is a gift of preparation and imagination from the storyteller to the audience. It is also a gift of shared appreciation from the audience to the storyteller. Such telling and listening to stories stimulates an interest in literature, strengthens language development, and primes the imagination.

One of the most personal ways of introducing literature to children is through *oral* story telling. Because there is no book separating you from your audience, there is an immediate contact and rapport. *An Exchange of Gifts: A Storyteller's Handbook* is for those who wish to share their favorite stories with children but are uncertain about how to begin. While the information contained within the text is based on personal experience, the material owes much to the teachers and students with whom I have come into contact during numerous storytelling sessions. Through their questions and comments, I have developed a practical approach by which a novice can develop skill in the area of storytelling.

The text offers encouragement as well as practical help. The bibliographies are intended to take the guesswork out of selecting books to share via storytelling. Consider them merely as starter lists, adding your own personal favorites as you discover new and exciting narratives to share.

Good storytelling!

Marion Ralston
New Westminster, B.C.
October 1991

THE BEGINNING

OF THE QUEST

"No! Tell us the story from *your* eyes!" A tiny hand partially obscured the first page of the book I was about to read to my class of first graders.

Glancing up I saw Jonathan, a usually docile and unassertive child, standing in front of me. While his plea evoked murmurs of approval and support from the other children, in me it inspired consternation and dismay. My storytelling experience, such as it was, had been confined to bedtime narratives for assorted nieces and nephews. These were a loyal, captive, largely uncritical, and wholly approving audience for whom the unpalatable alternative to an aunt's story was lights out.

"Not today Jonathan, but I promise we'll do it sometime soon," was my firm reply to the young child's request.

It took an investment of time and effort before I was able to keep my promise to Jonathan. Aided by a helpful children's librarian from the community centre, I began my storytelling odyssey with her recommendation for a beginning text: Ruth Sawyer's classic *The Way of the Storyteller*. Here I found a wealth of helpful material on selecting stories for an initial session, adapting printed material for storytelling, and choosing the right stories for special occasions.

Ruth Sawyer also suggests that, for the novice storyteller, the folk and fairy tales, plus the myths, legends and fables from traditional literature, are the easiest to tell because of their oral structures. Folk tales, for example, are composed of three distinct episodes which are easy to memorize.

Based on Sawyer's recommendations, my own first choice was 'The Musicians of Bremen', a traditional German tale collected by the Grimm brothers. This story of the cooperative efforts of a donkey, a hound, a cat and a rooster in routing a band of renegade robbers from the house in which the animals had taken shelter for the night proved to be an excellent choice. Because of its success, I went on to learn 'The Gingerbread Boy', 'Rumpelstiltskin'*, and 'The Three Billy Goats Gruff'.

I rapidly discovered that the elements which make these stories attractive to children are the very same ones which made them easy for me to learn. They have few major characters, an imaginative sequence of events, and simple direct language with many repetitions of key phrases. As a result, two of my major criteria for selecting stories are:

> i. minimum plot
> ii. maximum rhythm.

I also like the ones with delightful endings such as the two-line conclusion that is typical of Norwegian tales:

> "Snip, Snap, Snout
> This tale's told out!"

For older students, I find the Greek myths an invaluable resource. *Sun Flight* by Gerald McDermott concerns an engineering father who fashions wings of wax to help himself and his son escape from an island prison. Whenever I use it, this reworking of the Daedalus and Icarus legend provokes a lively discussion on the history of flight.

North American legends such as 'The Indian Cinderella' by Cyrus Macmillan and *The Fire Stealer* by William Toye are set in the heroic mode, and are of enduring interest and appeal to older students. Stories from African and Australian folklore make equally appropriate choices.

It's true that stories that have been told through the ages without losing their magic make ideal initial selections. But there are also many contemporary tales, such as *Jim and the Beanstalk* and *The True Story of the Three Little Pigs*, that are ideal for a storytelling session. In each selection, the artistry of the author's style

---

* Although I have had good success with 'Rumpelstiltskin', there are some people who believe that this is a racist tale. As a storyteller, you will have to be aware of the concerns expressed by ethnic, religious, and feminist groups, and consider whether or how you will use material which might cause them concern.

cries out to be shared with children, and I'm sure you'll prefer to read them aloud.

Don't confine yourself simply to reading stories, however. Although some stories are best read aloud, the time spent in learning a story is well worth it because storytelling offers a freedom that is never possible when one must continually refer to a book. For a young audience, even if the story you want to share is a picture book in which the illustrations are an important part of the story, it is helpful to know the narrative so well that you can allow your young audience an opportunity to enjoy the pictures to the full while you tell the story.

Finding good titles for a storytelling session *does* take some research. If you are unaware of the wealth of material now available, the search for suitable stories can be a pleasurable one. The world of children's literature offers wonderful tales that will give enjoyment to you as well as to your listeners. Ask the children's librarian at your public library to show you where to find the folk tales, the picture books, and the contemporary titles that are suitable for storytelling.

Stories suitable for an oral sharing usually depend upon action rather than description. "Once upon a time, in a land far away, there lived a boy named Jack . . ." This simple beginning introduces the main character who sets off on an adventure, becomes involved in a number of events, and eventually discovers both his fortune and his fate. Such stories have a logical sequence of events with no unnecessary descriptions. The narrative moves sequentially towards a climax, after which it may end quite abruptly as in "so they lived happily ever after." If no clear ending appears in the text, you may wish to conclude with something such as " . . and that was the story of The Princess on the Glass Hill."

Although the stories end, your children's delight in the tales you weave, and their growing appreciation of language, will continue long after today's students have gone on to become tomorrow's storytellers.

. . . .

STORYTELLING IN THE

LANGUAGE ARTS PROGRAM

T here is a natural bond between the oral sharing of stories and the goals of an effective Language Arts program. Both enhance communication in the oral and written forms, improve listening skills, instill an appreciation for good literature, and, best of all, assist in developing an active imagination.

ORAL COMMUNICATION:

Oral language is the foundation of a child's initial form of communication. Just as the storytellers of old shared the exploits of heroes, parents today share family memories, often in a narrative form. Children, in turn, frequently relate in a storytelling framework as they converse with friends. When the teacher provides a storytelling session for children, the literary material is often shared at home.

In a classroom setting, the teacher and students may discuss the merits of a shared story. The teacher can then stimulate discussion by posing leading questions. At other times, the students themselves may generate the conversation.

Sharing stories taught me a new way of reaching the students with whom I worked. After we had discussed a particular story, students often referred to it to help them describe a person or feeling. For example, "You know — like a Cinderella person" became a common phrase in my classroom. A few days after I read Judith Viorst's *Alexander and the Terrible, Horrible, No Good, Very Bad Day*, I noticed one of the boys with his feet dragging and his hands dug into his pockets. When he noticed me watching, he looked up, "Guess what, I'm having an Alexander day." We smiled at each other — in complete understanding.

I also discovered that the telling of a story requires a sharing of personal enthusiasm for a particular tale. *Never* try to tell a story which has little interest for you. This simply doesn't work, because the act of storytelling is one of reaching out and sharing something that you enjoy. When you, the storyteller, enjoy the story, it is never the same for it is created anew with each re-telling to a different audience.

Dr. Bruno Bettelheim in *The Uses of Enchantment: The Meaning and Importance of Fairy Tales* states that the telling of a story should be an interpersonal event into which adult and child enter as equal partners, as can never be the case when a story is read to a child. Interaction is also important to children when they are given the opportunity to join a refrain or to anticipate what a character will do when faced with a personal challenge. This is why the use of participation stories, and discussing what will happen to a character, are such important parts of the storytelling process. When such interaction is involved, children sense an intimate, caring relationship with the person telling the tale.

Children respond eagerly to the intimate warmth a storytelling session provides. They soon want to share their own selections with others. So begins a storytelling cycle that results in a searching out of new material and also an enthusiastic use of oral language. As a result, storytelling not only extends enjoyment of literature, it also helps students develop linguistic fluency, an important skill in our verbal society.

COMMUNICATION IN WRITTEN FORM:

Children's books offer excellent literary models for youngsters. They show how professional writers use language to create moods and images.

Folk tales, in particular, provide a treasure trove of material for children's written work. As children hear the familiar introductions to many of the tales: "Once upon a time . . .", "Once there was and once there was not . . . " or "Over a hill and far away in a beautiful land there lived a princess royal . . .", they begin to recognize that much of literature is predictable — and use some of the traditional patterns in their own writing.

Even very young children can learn to watch for a pattern of three. For example, many stories have three tasks to complete or three objects to be found, and this pattern often makes its way into their stories.

The conclusions, in which all ends happily ever after, also often find their way into children's written work, as do charming two-line summations such as:

Snip, snap, snover
This tale's over.

I have found that young children, in particular, become word-smiths when quality literature is shared with them. Many picture storybooks have the potential for stimulating an imaginative activity with words. A West African folk tale entitled *Why Mosquitoes Buzz in People's Ears* by Verna Aardema uses the Ashanti technique of repeating words and sounds for emphasis. Young children can pick up the book after their first oral encounter with the story and contribute their own original words and sounds in the appropriate places. Place a list of the children's creative word suggestions in the classroom library for future reference. Encourage older students to play with the Ashanti technique as they create their own folk tales.

Other titles suitable for similar activities include *Bimwilli and the Zimwi* and *The Crest and the Hide: Other African Stories*.

A book that is a perfect selection for involving children in creating original description is Barbara Cooney's *Chanticleer and the Fox*. Adapted from Chaucer's *Canterbury Tales*, the story contains an imaginative description of a proud rooster named Chanticleer. The author explains that Chanticleer's crowing is more trust-worthy than a clock, his comb redder than fine coral, his bill shining like jet, and his feathers of burnished gold. Children who have been introduced to this fanciful fowl can create a similar description of the fox, a wily character who appears later in the story.

LISTENING SKILLS:

Sharing narratives in which the events accumulate and then unravel helps children to master the skill of sequencing. Such tales as *One Fine Day, Drummer Hoff, The Gingerbread Boy, The Bremen Town Musicians* and 'Clever Elsie' (from *Womenfolk and Fairy Tales*) lend themselves well to this activity. If the teacher prefers, the stories may be taped and then replayed to check for accuracy.

For older students, a session in which they prepare stories for telling to younger children will assist in developing listening skills. Simple props such as a miniature spinning wheel to enhance a retelling of 'Sleeping Beauty', or a few shiny pebbles to highlight 'Hansel and Gretel', may assist novice storytellers in making their oral presentations. If the older students have prepared simple felt boards with accompanying illustrations, then the young listeners may be encouraged to retell the story as they place the visuals on the board in proper sequence.

Because of its many characters, *The Gingerbread Boy* is an excellent choice for felt board stories. My Junior level students prepared felt people and animals which they used in telling the story. Those that preferred the version in which the gingerbread boy is eaten by the fox also prepared a partially eaten gingerbread boy duplicate.

Another story that delights young storytellers is *Millions of Cats*, which was originally told to the author, Wanda Gag, by her German grandmother. One class of ten year olds that was fascinated by the tale worked with the Art teacher to make a series of woodcuts similar to Gag's illustrations. They used these woodcuts in sharing the story with a group of Primary students. The storytellers were enthusiastic; the audience was enthralled.

AN APPRECIATION OF GOOD LITERATURE:

When children and books come together, an interest in reading usually develops. The teacher who demonstrates her enthusiasm for books through a daily reading of a favorite novel or an oral retelling of a traditional tale inculcates in her students the spell of magic words.

Through storytelling sessions young children become aware of literature not otherwise available to them. Older children, who are more proficient at encoding and decoding skills, may be enticed into a novel by a storytelling introduction. That is why many librarians introduce starter novels by telling an exciting story about one of the characters. Students want to read the book to find out what happened.

For example, many Junior level students who hear about Lorinda's problems in earning enough money to buy a Christmas present for her mother will go on to read Budge Wilson's *The Worst Christmas Present Ever*. Frequently, they'll then read other stories about the Dauphinee family (*A House Far From Home*, and *Mystery Lights At Blue Harbour*), and may proceed to other books by the same author. Similarly, hearing how Dare is bored with a small town and listening to a smattering of his dialog, will entice many students into Marilyn Halvorson's *Dare*.

THE DEVELOPMENT OF AN ACTIVE IMAGINATION:

Youngsters develop their imaginative powers through the visualizations they create in their own minds. Without the artist's interpretation of a literary scene, they are free to imagine their own settings as the storyteller spins her tale. After hearing Danny Kaye read a favorite selection from the Grimm brothers, for example, one little pre-schooler remarked: "I like that! It (the tape) lets me make my own pictures in my mind."

For children, such involvement with literature results in a more personal interpretation of the storyteller's tale. This may be why books that depend essentially on illustration, such as James Herriot's *Oscar-Cat-About Town*, or on a specific writing style as found in Phoebe Gilman's *The Balloon Tree*, do not usually translate well into a spoken story form.

The written stories that *do* adapt well for telling have concise, action-filled plots that build toward a climax. These stories usually offer both drama and emotional appeal. *Tatterhood* by Robin Muller and *Mortimer* by Robert Munsch are two examples of books that translate well into an oral form. While the illustrations and the writing are well crafted, neither is essential to the narrative. The plots are interesting in themselves, making them good material for storytelling.

The genre of fantasy holds particular appeal for young listeners and is a wise choice for a beginning storyteller. This is because making the incredible seem credible stimulates the imagination. For this reason, young listeners enjoy the adventures and triumphs of traditional fairy tale characters. Such characters as 'Thorn Rose' (the original 'Sleeping Beauty' as told by the Grimm brothers), 'The Brave Little Tailor' (the Grimm brothers), and 'Yeh-Shen' (a Chinese version of the Cinderella tale), offer invitations to travel to horizons that do not exist in the children's real world.

DEVELOPMENT OF VOCABULARY:

The storyteller who uses rich, evocative language helps children to become aware of the power of words in conveying sensory images. Such language helps children view the world around them in new perspectives. For example, in *White Snow, Bright*

Snow, children hear that after an evening's snowfall:

> "Automobiles looked like big fat raisins buried in snowdrifts
> . . . and . . .
> Even the church steeple wore a pointed cap on its top."

Don't let archaic language deter your storytelling choices. Often the language peculiar to folk tales can be easily explained. In one story, the main character meets a lassie as he travels down a country road. By adding 'a young girl', the meaning becomes clear. Other words such as 'Goody' (old woman), 'minstrels' (musicians), and 'tapers' (candles) may also be explained with a casual reference.

It's interesting to note how often these words find their way into the children's own stories. The first phrase my Primary students adopted was "Once upon a time . . .". While these younger students were interested in the stories themselves, students ages 10 to 13 become intrigued with the origins of language and how words change from country to country. Often they would use typically British words to authenticate a British folk tale they were modernizing. In this way, gasoline became 'petrol'.

For Intermediate students, storytelling activities provide an opportunity for playing with language, and storytellers will do such things as changing 'Little Red Riding Hood' so that the wolf becomes a vegetarian. To motivate students to make such revisions, compare traditional fairy tale heroines with the one in Robert Munsch's *The Paperbag Princess*. Alternatively, discuss the usual version of 'Chicken Little', then read Steven Kellogg's version. Another interesting motivator is Susan Marcus's rap titled 'Nanny Goats Gruff' from the 'Dinosaur Tango' album.

APPRECIATION OF LITERATURE:

For many children, an appreciation of literature begins with the fun of the story. Humor is a quality that appeals to children of all ages. While the type of humor to which children respond does change, humor remains constant as a favorite choice for read and tell-aloud selections. Recommended authors of humorous material for younger children include Stephen Kellogg, Pat Hutchins and Bernard Waber. For older children try Beverly Cleary (the Ramona series), Robert McCloskey (the Homer Price series) and Robert Peck.

An appreciation of literature is based upon the pleasure of

hearing and/or reading stories. The enjoyment of an oral selection may be found in the content of the narrative or in the artistry of the author. Children who are caught up in the adventures of Homer Price, or by the melodic refrains of favorite folk tales, develop an interest in and an appreciation of many forms of literature.

The teacher, as storyteller, can enrich and enhance such experience. At the same time, through her own interest and enthusiasm for the activity, she can encourage her students to become storytellers.

FOLKLORE AND STORYTELLING:

My concern about whether some traditional stories, particularly those of the Grimm brothers, would disturb young listeners, led me to research the works of these German collectors. I found that their stories were intended, not for children, but for the archives of the University of Westphalia. When the first volume of *Kinder-und Hausmärchen (Nursery and Household Tales)* appeared in 1812, however, young and old delighted in the universal plots.

There are suspenseful stories of children turned out into a harsh world to fend for themselves (such as 'Hansel and Gretel') who find love and security after their hardships, and tales of dispossessed princes and princesses who retain their kindness and compassion (as in 'Beauty and the Beast'). In the Grimms' stories, children and youths respond to the challenge of great tasks and accomplish the impossible. Such stories make an ideal introduction to the literary world.

The stories found in folklore are rich in characterization, vocabulary and imagery. The narratives introduce students to global cultures and help children recognize that people all over the world are moved by the same emotions. Such stories have the power to give listeners insights into their own and others' behavior.

According to Dorothy Park and James Smith, two American researchers who put together a reference book on the importance of storytelling in the development of language, children find folk tales appealing for many reasons. First of all, the language is simple and direct. This makes it easier for young children to follow and understand the story.

Second, because plot is emphasized. While this offers a major advantage, namely of providing the amount of action that the listeners crave, it also has a major disadvantage. Like the stars in many modern films, the characters in folk tales tend to be stereotyped. Although stereotypical characters can cause social misconceptions, creative teachers can turn them into an advantage by using folk tales to help students recognize and analyze stereotypical behavior. For example, females who compare the passive heroines of folklore to the gutsy girls portrayed in such books as Katherine Paterson's *The Great Gilly Hopkins*, will recognize the full range of possible feminine behavior. Similarly, boys who see the cost of stereotypical male behavior, such as that shown in Budge Wilson's *Breakdown*, may begin to realize why it's important to express their emotions and needs. Alternatively, older students can compare folklore heroes to such modern creations as 'James Bond', 'Rambo', 'Dirty Harry', 'Crocodile Dundee' and 'MacGyver'. How are such characters one-sided? What purpose does this fulfil in the story or movie?

Third, because folk tales emphasize action. This immediately draws children into the story in the same way that an exciting chase scene or dramatic sports sequence attracts them to modern television. Fourth, folk tales also present and/or reinforce the basic values of a culture. Fifth, they help to meet the emotional needs of children, and stimulate young imaginations. Finally, many folk tales contain a subtle humor that children understand and enjoy.

In *The Uses of Enchantment: The Meaning and Importance of Fairy Tales*, Dr. Bruno Bettelheim writes that "to attain to the full its consoling propensities, its symbolic meanings, and most of all its interpersonal meanings, a fairy tale should be told rather than read." Dr. Bettelheim's words are echoed by professional storytellers such as Ruth Sawyer (*The Way of the Storyteller*), Marie Shedlock (*The Art of the Story-Teller*), and Jay O'Callahan (*A Master Class in Storytelling*).

Folk literature embodies universal themes of courage and wisdom common to all generations and thus transcends age barriers. Depending on the background of experience each child brings to any story, the narrative is interpreted in different personal ways. For the beginning storyteller, folk literature offers a practical narrative structure. For example, most stories have well-defined plots with a logical sequence of events. The characters are easily identified, the action is rapid, and the endings are usually satisfying.

Some novice storytellers wonder how fairy tales with gruesome endings will effect young listeners. This may have been a problem before the advent of modern television but now, with the amount of violence seen, in living color, right in their own homes, most children have a certain amount of tolerance for horror. As a result, I have found it rare for any child to be frightened by a story I'm telling. Usually, they seem to realize that this is a story and that everything will come out all right in the end. But if, as a storyteller, you are concerned about the effect a specific tale will have on a young audience, put the narrative aside. There are thousands of enchanting stories that will not upset young listeners.

If, however, you find yourself in the midst of sharing a tale when you realize that a child is frightened, walk casually to the youngster and place your hand gently on his/her shoulder. Smile reassuringly as you continue the story. Monitor the youngster's reactions as the story proceeds. Continue to offer warm reassurances by your smiles. What could have been an unpleasant experience can be turned into a positive encounter when you thus assist children in distancing themselves from a scary story in this way.

Advantages of Storytelling

When used by a sensitive teacher as part of the Language Arts program, storytelling has many important advantages.

1. ADAPTABILITY

Because you as the storyteller are in close communication with your listeners, you can adapt the content of your narrative — in midpassage if necessary. This technique is used to regain or retain interest in the story.

Adaptability is not confined to content. Each presentation must be geared to the mood and interests of your audience. For example, after great success reading *The Great Gilly Hopkins* to eleven year olds, one teacher moved on to Jan Truss's *Jasmin*. Although *Jasmin* is also about a female protagonist who is having problems, it is a more thoughtful book that didn't spark a response in the young listeners, possibly because of the number and length of descriptive passages. By condensing the description and emphasizing action, the teacher was able to help students appreciate this story.

2. COMMUNICATION

As the storyteller, you work *without* books or pictures. This leaves you free to concentrate on the narrative and to maintain eye contact with your audience. Use that eye contact to monitor the children's response to your tale. What parts delight them? At what point does their attention begin to wander? By using such audience feedback, Robert Munsch has developed a whole series of stories which enthral young audiences around the world. You can learn to do the same.

3. CHOICE OF MATERIAL

As the storyteller, you interpret and recreate material from traditional and contemporary sources, tailoring the language to the age of each particular group. Don't underestimate your audience. Children love to learn new words through the context of the storyteller's skill. To aid in their understanding, choose new words carefully. Use the phrase or sentence following the new word to explain what the introduced word means. This will assist students in learning to get word meaning from the context in which the word appears.

4. DRAMATIC INTERPRETATION

Because you are free to use a variety of facial expressions and body movements, you can enhance the dramatic elements. I found that by using a soft, slow and mysterious voice I could increase the tension in a suspenseful plot, while a livelier, brisker style proved better suited to action sequences.

Your Preparation for Storytelling

Such advantages depend on the storyteller's preparation. Yes, whether you're a novice or an experienced storyteller, it's important to prepare the story you're going to tell.

Know the story. Choose a story you like and with which you are comfortable. Read it over until you can remember the main points of the plot and can visualize the characters.

Analyze the story. What makes your choice of story an outstanding listening experience? Is it the plot, the characters, the dialog, or a combination of all three? Can your enthusiasm for the tale be transmitted in the telling? If you can't answer each of these questions, you're not ready to share a tale.

Re-read the story. A quick review of the narrative before you start telling it will refresh your memory on the main points of the plot, the special characteristics of the dialog, and the descriptive features of the characters.

Rehearse the story. Completing the first three steps, but going before your class without an oral rehearsal of the story, is like the musician who knows and appreciates a composer's work so well that he feels he need not practise it on his own instrument prior to a public performance. Only through practice can the storyteller know the best way to emphasize each segment of a particular narrative.

Practise raising and lowering your voice to create suspense and intrigue. Decide what body actions will enhance the telling of the tale. Plan how you will begin and end the story.

I found that a simple place and person introduction helps to establish the type of story. For example, "In a faraway land over the sea there once lived a king who had three sons . . .", or "Across the sky and behind the moon a special little girl was born . . ." Such openings introduce a simple setting and a few of the major characters.

Once the introduction is over, present the challenge faced by the protagonist/s. This could be an impending battle with a ferocious giant, a search for a lost treasure, or three impossible tasks. From here, the story progresses until the climax, during which the difficulty is resolved. Afterwards, the story reaches a conclusion.

During my initial storytelling sessions, I was unprepared for the questions and minor interruptions that arose. One little girl was so enthralled by the English folk tale 'Mollie Whuppie' that she exclaimed just before the conclusion: "Oh! Oh! How will Mollie every get away from the giant now?"

"Don't worry," Robbie, another child, reassured her. "She's smart. She'll find a way."

I found that by then saying, "Let's all listen and see if Robbie is right," I could draw the children back into the narrative. In fact, as my storytelling confidence increased, I started to welcome the children's interjections. They became an important and cherished aspect of storytelling participation.

Ways to Encourage Storytelling

In classrooms where children become fine storytellers, credit must go to the guidance of a sensitive teacher who has discovered that there are ways to encourage children to experiment with this traditional art form. Storytelling activities contribute to children's sense of narrative structure and content. Students learn that a story has a beginning, a middle, and an end. They also learn that in order to hold a listener's interest, the narrative must have action and evocative language. If children are encouraged through related activities, they can learn to tell stories and enjoy the satisfaction of creative oral expression.

The following list outlines a number of ways teachers can encourage storytelling within the classroom. Don't confine your experience to just one of these activities. Try to mix and match to give students a rounded approach to storytelling.

THE STORYTELLING CHAIR:

Following the recommendations of Marie Shedlock (*The Art of the Story-Teller*) and Eileen Colwell (*Storytelling*), I often share poetry, riddles and songs related to the story. The enrichment provided by this sharing encouraged greater participation and led to the creation of a storytelling chair. This article of furniture was donated by a generous custodian who found a small and neglected rocking chair which he painted a brilliant gold. He then pasted a hand-lettered sign above it: 'This is a Magic Storytelling Chair. All are Welcome.'

Students were invited to sit in the chair and tell a story, recite a poem, or share a joke or riddle with whomever constituted their audience. It was as I watched the children responding to this magical environment, and then taking their own first steps as storytellers, that I became convinced that every child's experience must include this art.

THE STORYTELLING CORNER:

In addition to the magic chair, I created a storytelling corner furnished with a small, soft rug. To increase the size of the area, I presented each child with a carpet square generously donated by a local shop. A framed Norman Rockwell print of 'The Storyteller' placed above a shelf of books completed the corner.

STORYTELLING MUSIC:

When storytelling time was about to begin, I alerted the children by playing 'The Teddybears' Picnic' on a miniature music box. When the children heard the melodic refrain of this well-known tune, they gathered at the storytelling corner ready for enchantment.

LISTENING TO ORAL STORIES:

Listening to others tell stories gives children an example to follow. If the narratives are of the participation type (see Appendix C, page 45), the children will imitate the chants, the dialog, the new words and the ways in which the storyteller uses language as they retell their own versions.

SHARING STORIES:

Show-and-Tell gives children a chance to talk about a specific object held in the hand. Children can begin with as simple a statement as ''This is my favorite toy car.'' As they gain in skill and poise the stories will lengthen and become more complex. Remind the children to plan what they will say about what they have brought. For variety they may *write* their information and *read* it to the class. Encourage the other students to ask questions.

CHORAL SPEAKING:

Repeating rhymes, chants, and poems in unison with the teacher, or repeating parts of a poem, gives children confidence and poise. Contrasting voices could take solo parts or refrains.

GROUP CO-OPERATIVE STORIES:

Contributing individual ideas about a specific group topic helps children to realize that their ideas are important. The group efforts can be placed on a chart or put into book form.

STORYTELLING GAMES:

'I went shopping and I bought _____.' The next player adds another item, then repeats all the previous items in order:

    Player One: 'I went shopping and I bought a new doll.'
    Player Two: 'I went shopping and I bought a new doll and a rocking horse.'

Player Three: 'I went shopping and I bought a new doll, a rocking horse, and a Dinky toy.'

This activity helps children to sequence events, an important characteristic of successful storytelling.

READING PICTURES:

Pictures can give children ideas about which they can talk. Reading the action in one picture, or a sequence of pictures, and telling what happened before and after helps children develop the ability to tell stories. Cartoons without dialog such as the old 'Nipper' series, advertising flyers, and magazine photos make ideal selections for this activity. Many younger children particularly enjoy the action shots used in outdoor, equestrian, hunting, and fishing magazines.

CREATIVE DRAMATICS:

Dramatizing simple stories gives children vivid mental pictures. One primary teacher got excellent results using Freya Littledale's *The Magic Fish*, a tale about a greedy wife who sends her husband to demand more and more from a magic fish that he has saved. Children enjoy playing the husband reeling in the fish. They love talking like the imperious wife, and delight in the repeated refrain:

> "Oh fish of the sea
> Come listen to me
> My wife begs a wish
> From the magic fish."

It is a natural step from portraying a story through movement to telling a story with words. Often students will move from acting out a story to writing it down. This procedure is particularly important when working with Special Education students with limited verbal skills, and in English As A Second Language classrooms.

SENSORY EXPERIENCES:

The use of vivid words in storytelling is based on strong sensory impressions that are gained through experience. Make a 'feeling' box out of an old hat box with an opening in the lid, or by gluing the top of an old sock to the mouth of a large juice can. Children reach in to touch a bit of satin, fur, sandpaper, felt, and other materials. To help build a meaningful vocabulary, chart the words they use to describe how the objects feel.

I am a strong believer that literature is like a database. It provides children with new words and ways to use them. For example, after hearing Beatrix Potter's *The Tale of Benjamin Bunny*, one six-year-old explained, "I'm going to bed early tonight because I feel very soporific."

Words are the tools of a storyteller. This helps children learn new vocabulary, new meanings for words, and new ways of using language. Encourage them to try out new words and expressions, and to act out the meanings of new words in order to make them concrete. Continue to help them stretch for new vocabulary by using advanced words followed by a brief explanation. Long before the word 'extinct' was in common usage, Hugh Lofting had his Dr. Dolittle point out that push-me pull-yous are now extinct. Within a few lines, the meaning of the word was made clear. Follow the same practice when using a new or difficult word.

PUPPETS:

A puppet theatre with costumes, props, and space for a few children to recreate familiar stories will provide a good foundation for encouraging an interest in storytelling. Shy children tend to be less inhibited and more imaginative when using puppets while telling a tale.

Don't confine puppet theatres to the youngest students; older students can also benefit from using them. When several eleven year old students rewrote *The Wizard of Oz* as a play, they produced a series of puppets, including an aluminum foil 'tin' woodman, complete with a door in his chest that revealed a heart. Using these props, they retold the story for delighted young listeners.

TALKING ABOUT STORYTELLING:

Discuss the simple elements of a good story: action, suspense, emotion, conversation and sensory appeal. Develop class charts listing the children's favorite words, characters, and plots, plus the reasons for their choices.

Books such as John Green's *There's a Dragon in My Closet* will help some students identify the elements of humor, surprise, and repetition. Encourage students to bring their favorite books from home. Read and/or tell them to the class. Discuss what makes them so appealing.

CRITIC'S CORNER:

Children can be encouraged to tell a part of a story they have liked to their classmates. They can also tape-record their analytical opinions of particular books they have read, and place tapes in a library or book corner for others to hear.

Confine such criticism to professionally written stories. Children need to greet each others's efforts with enthusiasm and praise; otherwise, the spark of a beginning storyteller may be snuffed out.

. . . .

A STARTER LIST OF
RECOMMENDED TYPES OF
ORAL STORIES

PARTICIPATION STORIES:

In participation stories, the teacher shares the main part of the narrative. The children participate by repeating a chant, by adding body actions, or by contributing a final word to end a rhyming couplet. This activity is enjoyed by young as well as older students.

Participation stories may be adapted from familiar folk tales or from any story to which creative actions and/or sounds can be added. The success of participation stories depends on the active involvement of children in the storytelling session. Start with titles such as *The Wheels on the Bus* by Maryann Kovalski, *Could Be Worse!* by James Stevenson, or *Hush Little Baby* by Margot Zemach.

One day I shared Marjorie Flack's *Ask Mr. Bear*, in which a little boy asks a succession of animals for their suggestions for a birthday present he plans to give his mother. The surprise ending, when Mr. Bear provides the perfect solution of a big, birthday bear hug, delighted the children. After school several of them remained behind to help tidy the classroom, leaving me time to print reading questions for the following day's lesson on the blackboard.

With my back to the children, I failed to realize that I was about to become the recipient of a huge bear hug usually reserved for grandparents bearing gifts. The chalk flew out of one hand, my list of questions out of the other. With a pounding heart I turned to find the shyest child, arms outstretched, waiting for his return bear hug. And so my classroom had, through storytelling, been touched and warmed by an added dimension of love, and had indeed witnessed an exchange of gifts.

PICTURE STORIES:

In this type of activity, the story is told by following the illustrations. Young children enjoy stories about talking animals, make-believe and everyday experiences to which they can relate. When sharing such stories, make sure that the group is small enough to gather around and see the pictures. Practise the narrative until you are so familiar with the story that you can share it while holding the book facing the children. (See Chapter 4: 'Stories To Read Aloud'.)

For starters, try Virginia Burton's *Mike Mulligan and His Steam Shovel*, *Blueberries for Sal* by Robert McCloskey, or Allen Morgan's *Matthew and the Midnight Tow Truck*.

FOLK TALES FROM OTHER LANDS:

Most children are introduced to storytelling through the traditional literature of old. The folk and fairy tales, myths, legends and fables all form a body of literature that has been spoken and passed by word of mouth from one reteller to the next. Because traditional literature contains themes that are timeless and universal in their appeal, the stories speak as much to the children of today as they did to those of yesteryear.

Start with:

East of the Sun and West of the Moon by P. Asbjornsen and J. Moe.
Once More Upon A Totem by Christie Harris.
The Arabian Nights by P. Colum.
Stone Soup by Ann McGovern.
The Story of King Arthur and His Knights by Howard Pyle.
Womenfolk and Fairy Tales Rosemary Minard ed.

My storytelling activities extended beyond my classroom when, at the principal's request, I instituted fifteen minute storytelling sessions for the children waiting for the afternoon school bus. On one occasion, with St. Patrick's Day fast approaching, I chose to share the cycle of stories from *The King of Ireland's Son* by Padraic Colum. The following day, while supervising the playground, I felt a tiny hand slip into mine, and heard a tremulous little girl's whisper ask, "Please, I was sick at home yesterday. Is the little princess awake yet?"

As I looked down into her earnest little face, I thought of the concluding lines from Virginia Tashjian's collection of Armenian tales, *Three Apples Fell From Heaven: Armenian Tales Retold*: "One for the storyteller, one for the listener, and one for the one who truly heard."

"Yes," I softly replied, "the little princess is awake now. Would you like to hear the rest of the story?"

. . . .

STORIES TO READ

ALOUD

Although oral storytelling is an excellent way to introduce children to literature, there are some stories that should be read rather than told. These are the narratives in which the author has used language so evocatively that not to share the words as they were written would do a disservice to both the writer and the listener. Experience will help you identify these stories when you try them aloud. You will become aware of descriptive passages and complex sentence structures which read well but would be difficult to memorize.

Literary versions of fairy tales such as the stories retold by Charles Perrault, Hans Christian Andersen, and Andrew Lang come into this category. The tales of Rudyard Kipling in his *Just So Stories* and *The Jungle Book* are a delight to read aloud because of his creative use of words. Beatrix Potter, with her stories of 'soporific' bunnies and birds who 'implore' Peter to exert himself, is another wordsmith whose works deserve to be read as they are.

Playful language, in which authors invent or use words or idioms, also needs to be read aloud. A. A. Milne in his delightful Winnie The Pooh stories, and Michael Bond with his Paddington Bear series, as well as writers such as Edward Lear, and Lewis Carroll, all employ inventive language and, at times, have the main character take the wrong meanings from the directives given to them. Peggy Parish's Amelia Bedelia stories revolve around one character misunderstanding the phrasing used by the others. Such plays on words are difficult to do without reading the original text.

Stories which have been written to convey mood or attitude,

or in which there is more description than action, are usually better read. Remember that reading a story well requires just as much care and preparation as does telling a story.

Your Selection and Preparation for Reading Aloud

Reading aloud to children of all ages creates a communal bond. When students are caught up in the excitement of an adventure story, or in the satisfying conclusion to an intriguing mystery, they share in a universal literary experience.

To increase interest in the selection to be read aloud, preface it with a short poem or newspaper article relating to the story. For example *The Incredible Journey*, by Sheila Burnford, relates the odyssey of a golden labrador, a bull terrier and a siamese cat across 400 kilometres of Northern Ontario bush in order to find their way back home. A short poem from one of Lee Bennett Hopkins' anthologies, or a brief newspaper article about animal survival, could introduce the novel.

To help students fully experience the power of the stories you're reading, create a pleasant atmosphere.

"The story candle is lit and now the magic begins."

That's how one teacher prefaces each read-aloud and storytelling session. The colored story candle is housed in a hurricane-type lamp for safety reasons and is extinguished by a child volunteer at the conclusion of the activity. The charming custom of the lighting of the candle delights the children, who look forward to this little ritual each time it is performed.

If possible, have an area where a story circle can be created. Gather the children around you, ensuring that all can see any illustrations.

Select a story with your students in mind. Personal observation of their activities and a review of their interest inventories (see Appendix A, page 39) will assist you in deciding what to choose to read aloud. In general, young children enjoy stories about funny animals, folk and fairy tales, and children who live in a realistic world like their own. Older students appreciate adventure, mystery, nature and science fiction.

Before making a choice, it's important to consider your students' cultural background. One of my friends had used *Charlotte's Web* for years. When she began teaching English As A Second Language, however, she noticed that some of her students were completely bored by this old favorite. Upon discussing this attitude with her East Indian charges, she learned that they couldn't understand why a pig, no matter how clever, would be so revered that it wouldn't be killed for meat. Similarly, some of your favorites may not be able to cross cultural barriers.

Choose a book that *you* enjoy. The enthusiasm you have for the narrative will be conveyed to the students through your voice. A good book for children should appeal to adults, particularly the storyteller. C.S. Lewis, the author of the Narnia Series, believed that a book worth reading at the age of ten was equally worth reading at the age of fifty.

Rehearse. Preview your selection by skimming through the story ahead of time. This rehearsal will alert you to the author's style and to the basic theme or concept of the narrative. In becoming familiar with the content of the book you allow for more eye contact with the children, an important technique in sustaining the interest of young listeners.

Introduce the author. Students need to learn about the creators of children's literature and why they write as they do. By so doing, teachers help children to develop an understanding of books as living literature. On occasion, biographical sketches about the authors will be found on the dust jackets of their respective titles. If this information is not available, professional sources will give you interesting anecdotes to share with a class. Helpful references in this field include *Books Are By People* by Lee Bennett Hopkins, and *Something About The Author* by Anne Commire. For Canadian authors, refer to Barbara Greenwood's *Presenting Children's Authors, Illustrators and Performers*, or the Canadian Children's Book Centre (35 Spadina Road, Toronto, Ontario, M5R 2S9), which publishes biography sheets as well as videos on well-known Canadian writers and illustrators for young people.

. . . .

STORYTELLING

ACTIVITIES

Children's understanding of literature is enhanced if they have the opportunity to interact with the narrative. For example, at the conclusion of a story, the students may interpret the theme or plot through improvised drama presentations, a discussion about a main character's actions, or through a music and/or art activity. For many children, new perspectives about the literature selection are shared as the students hear or see how their classmates have interpreted the intent of the author.

The following recommended activities may be used in any order and, with a few exceptions, are suitable for children of all ages. Like storytelling itself, their purpose is to enhance the students' appreciation and enjoyment of literature.

A STORY, A STORY:

How did stories originate? The answer is retold by Gail Haley in a delightful African folk tale, *A Story, A Story*. From this narrative, children gain an understanding of the importance of storytelling in the African culture. Similarly useful is Lucillena Clifton's *The Lucky Stone*, which highlights a family's tradition of storytelling as a young girl hears her great grandmother's stories.

Tales From The Story Hat: African Folktales also reinforces the importance of the oral transmission of traditional tales. Each of the nine stories is represented by an object dangling from the storyteller's hat. When a listener selects an item, the storyteller recounts the related story. A classroom story hat made from a straw boater or some similar design could be created with items representing the students' favorite narratives.

An individual or group storytelling journal can record the children's responses toward the tales told aloud. Written critiques by the students, their illustrations of favorite incidents, and listings of new vocabulary learned from the narratives may be incorporated. If replies have been received from authors to whom children have written, the information along with biographical sketches of the writers may be included.

STORY MAP:

A large world map can be posted near the storytelling corner. As favorite folk and fairy tales are shared, their origins can be pinpointed by colored stickers or miniature flags representing the respective countries. Such characters as 'Cinderella' (France), the 'Three Billy Goats Gruff' (Norway), 'Glooscap' (Canada), 'Snow White' (Germany) and 'Molly Whuppie' (England) will show the universality of folklore.

STORY MURALS:

Favorite fable characters such as the 'Lion' and the 'Mouse', or the 'Hare' and the 'Tortoise' may motivate children to create a mural depicting the morals associated with each narrative. Balloon blurbs, as illustrated by Alice and Martin Provensen in Louis Untermeyer's *Aesop's Fables*, can be used for the message statements.

STORY BULLETIN BOARDS:

Students can create a series of bulletin boards emphasizing a particular literary genre. If traditional tales are chosen for this activity, cultural variants can be highlighted. Many older children are intrigued to discover that some stories appear in almost every culture.

According to Mary Anne Nelson, an American university professor who wrote a comparative anthology of children's literature, over five hundred versions of the Cinderella story have been found throughout the world. She suggests that the original story began in Asia, spread from there to Egypt, and was brought to Germany and France during the Middle Ages by merchants.

Encourage students to take a look at several variations on the Cinderella tale. Discuss how and why the heroine's name may change from country to country. For example, she is also referred to as 'Tattercoats' (England), 'The Serf Among the Ashes' (Germany), 'Little Burnt Face' (Canada) and 'Little Red Shoes' (Egypt). In the original, the step-sisters mutilate their feet in order to try to fit them into the tiny slipper. The French storyteller Charles Perrault, who heard the original tale as a child, changed this part in the modern versions.

Provide bulletin board space for children's advertisements of favorite stories. Students who have read Eric Carle's *The Very Hungry Caterpillar* delight in finding ways to illustrate items that have been eaten by caterpillars. Placing these on a bulletin board or other display advertising Eric Carle's work encourages other children to enjoy his stories.

What images spring to mind when you hear a book title such as *Can You Teach Me To Pick My Nose* by Martin Godfrey? Encourage older students to develop posters illustrating the dual meaning in this title. Use them to advertise the book. Similarly, fish models or a tack display could advertise Sharon Siamon's *Fishing for Trouble*.

SEQUENCE ACTIVITY:

A sequential activity to help students become more aware of plot development may be organized around a participation bulletin board. Children's illustrations from a story told aloud can be mounted on oak tag or bristol board and placed, in random order, in a heavy envelope. The pictures can then be matched to printed descriptions numbered in order.

DRAMATIZATION:

Stories from the myths provide useful material for classroom dramatization. *King Midas And The Golden Touch, The Warrior Goddess*, and *The Hammer of Thunder* all lend themselves to creative interpretation.

Older students may prefer to act out scenes from a favorite novel. Sylvia McNicoll's *Project Disaster* has some hilarious scenes that younger students will relish, while intermediate students may be more interested in recreating the conflict between the three teenagers in Karleen Bradford's *Windward Island*.

FOLKLORE AND FANCIES:

To create an interest in a story you are about to tell, hold an object in your hand that is related to the narrative. For example, a paper party hat could introduce *The Five Hundred Hats of Bartholomew Cubbins,* or a few white pebbles could highlight the story of 'Hansel and Gretel'. The following list suggests objects and the stories they represent:

ITEM	RELATION	STORY
a red pebble	a magic stone capable of granting wishes	*Sylvester and the Magic Pebble* (Steig)
a fresh or silk flower	an appreciation of wisdom and beauty	*The Girl Who Cried Flowers* (Yolen)
a story box	how stories came into existence	*A Story, A Story* (Haley)
a miniature spinning wheel	a means of casting a hundred year spell	'The Sleeping Beauty' (Grimm)
a glossy feather	an ingenious method of escape	*Sun Flight* (McDermott)

Encourage students to search for suitable objects to introduce the stories they will tell as their storytelling experiences progress.

FICTION AND FOOD:

Used sparingly, a special treat of an edible item associated with a story will delight children. For example, a bowl of fresh blueberries may be shared after telling Robert McCloskey's *Blueberries For Sal,* while sandwiches and a surprise party could introduce *Bread and Jam For Frances* by Russell Hoban. Older students will enjoy homemade doughnuts as described in the story titled "The Doughnuts" from Robert McCloskey's *Homer Price.*

GUEST STORYTELLERS:

Invite storytellers from the community to share their favorite narratives. Many senior citizens have wonderful memories about school days and local geographical areas where modern development has since occurred. The school 'family' of the principal, secretary, and custodian could also take part in sharing memories of childhood storytelling sessions. If there is a First Nations Reserve near the school, invite native storytellers to share some of their traditional tales. Alternatively, ask members of a local ethnic community to share the richness of their heritage.

After listening to some of the tales told by Scheherazade in *The Arabian Nights*, encourage students to spin their own magic. Discuss the selection of a story and what makes it a good choice for oral telling (a strong beginning, rapid action, few characters and a satisfying conclusion).

Have students practise with a tape recorder or tell their stories in small groups. Volunteers who feel confident about their storytelling abilities may then share their stories with the entire class or with a group of younger children.

AUTHOR WEEK:

A week of storytelling highlighting the works of one particular author could reinforce the literary contributions made by gifted writers.

The birthdays of authors may also be celebrated on a weekly or monthly basis. Some writers whose works are suitable for storytelling include:

Hugh Lofting	Dr. Dolittle series	January 14
Howard Pyle	Robin Hood	March 5
Hans Christian Andersen	fairy tales	April 2
Beverley Cleary	Ramona series	April 12
James Barrie	*Peter Pan*	May 9
Maurice Sendak	*Where The Wild Things Are*	June 10
Beatrix Potter	*The Tales of Peter Rabbit*	July 28
Roald Dahl	*Charlie and the Chocolate Factory*	September 13
William Cole	*Oh, Such Foolishness!*	November 20
Rudyard Kipling	*The Jungle Book*	December 30

Encourage Intermediate students to compare traditional fairy tales with the way Walt Disney portrays the same story. Because Disney's cartoon version is so easily available on VHS, the Scandinavian story of 'The Little Mermaid' might be a good place to start this activity. How are the traditional and modern stories the same? How are they different? Why?

MODERN PARALLELS:

For older students, a research activity to find mythic parallels in the modern world could lead to an understanding that mythology still lives. The ancient myths dealt with people's fears and desires. Encourage students to analyze television programs to see what modern fears and desires are being expressed. For example, how many dramas revolve around doctors and/or hospitals? Is this a reference to our worries about health? How many spy and police shows are popular because of a typical wish that law and order will vanquish crime? What sitcoms depend on our desire for families in which father usually knows best (such as The Cosby Show and Full House)?

How are myths used in advertising? For example, how many products are named after a god or goddess? Discuss the frequent use of Mercury, Pluto, Aphrodite, and Hermes in company or product names. How many use Zeus's thunderbolt or Poseidon/Pluto's trident as a symbol? How many refer to unicorns or other mythical creatures?

What companies depend on modern myths to advertise their products? For example, Ultra-brite toothpaste sells cleanliness, blue jeans sell the frontier, and Green products sell concern for the environment. How is Cadbury's using mythology to advertise its Caramilk bar? Particularly note the ads referring to Elvis Presley and James Dean. How is each of these men an example of a modern myth? For help, students might want to read an issue of 'The National Enquirer', which depends on mythology to garner a gigantic readership. Note the number of stories about contact by creatures from other planets, tales of people who are incredibly disfigured, and constant references to movie idols and royalty, the modern equivalent of mythical heroes and heroines.

What modern movies revolve around characters that seem invincible? Which ones depend on a sex object? Rambo, for example, could be compared with Mars, the god of war. Marilyn

Monroe is the best-known example of a modern Aphrodite.

Many cult figures, such as Madonna, depend on mythology. Madonna's name is based on Christian mythology. Do her dress and actions reflect or contradict the name she chose? What do other idols, such as Michael J. Fox, Corey Hart, and New Kids on the Block represent? What basic needs do they fulfil?

Teachers and students particularly interested in this field might want to contact The Association of Media Literacy (40 McArthur Street, Weston, Ontario, M9P 3M7), which publishes a newsletter and a series of media activities, some of which deal with mythology in the media.

CONCLUSION:

If you want to be a storyteller, you must be prepared to work at it. It takes time to search for appropriate material and to get to know your selections. I've provided the listings of recommended books and their annotations to help you, as a beginning storyteller, to reach out and select materials quickly and easily. I've also included additional enrichment suggestions to enhance your children's enjoyment of storytelling.

Remember that storytelling is well worth all your efforts at preparation and presentation. It is an easy and satisfying way to introduce books to children and to give pleasure to them.

Children will respond to a wide range of themes, ideals and emotional situations presented in the stories you tell them. Never underestimate the ability of your students to understand allegorical material. It could be said of modern fantasy such as *Charlotte's Web*, the Wizard of Oz *(The Land of Oz)*, and *The High King* that ''the words are for children but the meanings are for men.'' Discussion of such stories will help students — both the younger ones, and you, the storyteller, to grow.

By encouraging students to participate in activities designed to extend their appreciation of the stories told aloud, you, as the teacher, help to create a lasting interest in literature. It's not easy. Sharing stories through reading and telling means giving something of yourself. Through your words and gestures you shape a literary experience for children.

The tools are simple. All that you need to start are your interest, your memory, your voice and a story, old or new. Remember that good stories are like gifts. The sharing of them makes for very special moments which will never be forgotten.

APPENDICES

. . . .

APPENDIX A

Interest Inventory

Interest and reading inventories such as the following can provide useful data about your students' after school activities, hobbies, sports, and television shows. For children who are too young to read or write their responses, an adult or older child may record the answers.

NAME: _____ AGE: _____

1. What do you like to do after school?

2. Do you have a pet at home? If so, what kind?

3. What hobbies or collections do you have?

4. What sports do you like?

5. What are your favorite television shows?

6. What do you like to do on Saturday?

7. Where would you like to go on a vacation?

8. What board games do you like best?

9. Which school subject do you like the best? Why?

10. List your favorite movies.

Reading Inventory

1. Do you have a library card?

2. Do you own any books? Approximately how many? What are some of the titles?

3. What things do you like to read about?

4. Do you have a subscription to a magazine? If so, which one/s?

5. Name a book you would like to read again. Why?

. . . .

APPENDIX B

Professional Bibliography

If you give children pleasurable experiences with words through storytelling, you will create life-long devotees of literature. The following list is intended as a beginning resource.

Aubrey, Irene (1984). *Storyteller's Encore.* Toronto: Canadian Library Association.
  As in *Storyteller's Rendezvous* (1979), this collection contains folk tales, legends, and poems ideal for a beginner's storytelling session. The amount of time required to tell a story, and the age suitability of each selection, are also included.

Baker, Augusta and Ellin Greene (1987). *Storytelling: Art and Technique.* 2nd. edition. New York: Bowker.
  Two gifted storytellers share their personal experiences, and discuss and outline basic storytelling techniques for the beginner.

Barton, Bob (1986). *Tell Me Another: Storytelling and Reading Aloud at Home, at School, and in the Community.* Markham, Ontario: Pembroke Publishers.
  The author provides a useful reference for storytelling and reading aloud techniques whether at home, at school, or in a community setting. The book includes practical suggestions on getting started, and a fine selection of stories.

Barton, Bob and David Booth (1990). *Stories in the Classroom.* Markham, Ontario: Pembroke Publishers.
  This helpful text makes recommendations for enriching school curriculum through storytelling. The authors stress the importance of stimulating the imaginative and visualization abilities of children through selected stories.

Bauer, C. (1985). *Celebrations: Read-Aloud Holiday and Theme Book Programs*. New York: Wilson.
    An excellent resource for creative program ideas and storytelling techniques to celebrate special occasions, seasons, and holidays. Suggested activities include ideas for poetry, puppetry, and creative drama sessions.

Bettelheim, Bruno (1967). *The Uses of Enchantment: The Meaning and Importance of Fairy Tales*. New York: Knopf.
    This basic text defines how children respond to literature. It suggests that folktales do far more than entertain; they also enhance a child's imagination.

Colwell, Eileen (1983). *Storytelling*. London: Bodley Head.
    A more formal approach to storytelling is offered in this helpful reference. Teacher/librarians in the school system would find the detailed information useful in planning programs for children. The contents include an in-depth discussion on the values of oral literature, the process of finding a suitable story, and the practice required to share it effectively with various age levels of children. Although the book is currently out of print, it is still available in some libraries.

Commire, Anne (1971). *Something About The Author*. Detroit, Michigan: Gale Research.
    An excellent resource, this series provides biographical information about authors and illustrators of books for young people.

Egoff, Sheila, ed. (1980). *Only Connect: Readings On Children's Literature*. Don Mills, Ontario: Oxford.
    In this useful book of history and criticism, especially note 'On Three Ways of Writing for Children' by C. S. Lewis.

Greenwood, Barbara, ed. (1991). *Presenting Children's Authors, Illustrators and Performers* Markham, Ontario: Pembroke Publishers.
    Outlines profiles of 37 Canadian artists as written by their peers. Each profile contains biographical information as well as a discussion of the individual's work and creative contributions to the field.

Harrell, John (1983). *Origins and Early Traditions of Story-Telling*. Kensington, California: York House.

Storytelling, the art behind traditional literature, had its beginnings in antiquity. Harrell traces the development of storytelling and shares a number of interesting anecdotes related to early techniques. This reference is suggested for the experienced storyteller.

Hopkins, Lee Bennett (1969). *Books Are by People*. New York: Citation.

This volume outlines interviews with more than one hundred authors and illustrators of books for young children. Although the book is currently out of print, it is still available in larger libraries that specialize in material for children.

Livo, Norma and Sandra Rietz (1987). *Storytelling: Process and Practice*. Littleton, Colorado: Libraries Unlimited.

The authors introduce practical means by which the reader can develop skill in the art of storytelling. This book is meant to appeal to the totally inexperienced teller of stories who needs quickly and easily to identify appropriate material.

MacDonald, Margaret, ed. (1982). *The Storyteller's Sourcebook: A Subject, Title and Motif Index to Folklore Collections for Children*. Detroit, Michigan: Gale Research Inc.

Intended for the most serious student of folklore, this volume offers an extensive listing of titles and motifs. Because it provides access to titles usually found only in general collections, this reference is particularly useful to teacher/librarians.

Maguire, Jack (1985). *Creative Storytelling: Choosing, Inventing, and Sharing Tales for Children*. New York: McGraw-Hill.

Helpful guidance is offered from a thoughtful expert who discusses the importance of reading aloud to children, as well as sharing literature in a storytelling session. The author outlines creative techniques he has found useful in becoming a successful storyteller.

Marcus, Susan (1988). 'Nanny Goats Gruff' from April and Susan's 'Dinosaur Tango'. Willowdale, Ontario: Join In Music.

Through an amusing and up-beat rap, Susan Marcus retells the story of the 'Three Billy Goats Gruff'. The conclusion, in which the troll becomes a vegetarian, will inspire older listeners to try their own modernized versions of favorite fairy tales.

O'Callahan, Jay (1983). *A Master Class in Storytelling*. New York: Vineyard Video.

This helpful resource uses video to show some of the techniques that just can't be explained in writing.

Sawyer, Ruth (1977). *The Way of the Storyteller*. New York: Penguin.
A classic in the field of storytelling, Sawyer's book offers sound advice on selection and presentation. Extensive bibliographies add to the value of this helpful guide for the beginning storyteller.

Shedlock, Marie L. (1951). *The Art of the Story-Teller*. New York: Dover.
This reference contains essential material for the novice storyteller who needs assistance in locating, adapting, and creating stories for children. Includes helpful techniques in presenting stories and useful bibliographies.

Yolen, Jane (1981). *Touch Magic: Fantasy, Faerie and Folklore in the Literature of Children*. New York: Putnam.
For the more advanced student of storytelling, this reference contains essays on the importance of fantasy in stimulating the imagination and acquiring language. The author stresses the sharing of folk literature as it began; that is, in a storytelling form.

APPENDIX C

A Starter List of Participation Titles

Participation stories are those in which the listeners join in the storytelling. Once you and your students realize the joy and excitement of such involvement, you will want to make participation stories part of your regular storytelling menu.

Read-aloud stories can also be exciting, especially when the story-teller has used some of the techniques outlined in Chapter 4: 'Stories To Read Aloud'. That's why the list of participation titles is followed by two lists, one of read-aloud books for younger children, the second of ones for older children.

Ahlberg, Janet and Allan Ahlberg (1989). *Bye Bye Baby*. London: Heinemann.
> In this charming fantasy, a baby who has no family goes in search of a mother to help him with his daily life. Because he does not know what a mother looks like, the baby finds himself involved in amusing situations with unusual mother-type characters.

Allen, Pamela (1990). *I Wish I Had A Pirate Suit*. New York: Viking Penguin.
> Peter's wish comes true and his fantastic seafaring adventures are told in narrative rhyme.

Aylesworth, Jim (1989). *Mr. McGill Goes To Town*. New York: Henry Holt.
> Mr. McGill enlists the aid of several of his neighbors in order to finish his chores in time to go into town. The cumulative pattern to the story is a traditional one.

Base, G. (1990). *My Grandma Lived In Gooligulch*. New York: Abrams.

Australia is the setting for this delightful story of an eccentric grandmother who shares her house with an assortment of unusual animals.

Brown, R. (1985). *The Big Sneeze*. New York: Lothrop, Lee & Shepard Books.
The consequences of a sneeze and its results on a farmer, his wife and the animals all contribute to a hilarious climax.

Burton, Virginia L. (1939). *Mike Mulligan and His Steam Shovel*. Boston: Houghton Mifflin.
The modern problem of obsolescence is solved in an ingenious way when Mike helps his faithful steam shovel to a new life.

Carle, Eric (1969). *The Very Hungry Caterpillar*. New York: Philomel.
What does a caterpillar do when it is very hungry? Children will be amused with the simple text and wonderful illustrations of this storyteller, who has produced a series of useful books including *Have You Seen My Cat?* (1988) and *Do You Want To Be My Friend?* (1971).

Cooney, Barbara (1985). *Miss Rumphius*. New York: Penguin.
Miss Rumphius' childhood search for something to make the world more beautiful extends over a lifetime. At last she finds fulfilment in her village by the sea. The narrative embodies a poignant message for all listeners.

Dabcovich, Lydia (1982). *Sleepy Bear*. New York: Dutton.
The signs of a changing season are explored in this charming book as Sleepy Bear prepares for his winter hibernation.

Flack, Marjorie (1958). *Ask Mr. Bear*. New York: Macmillan.
A little boy asks a succession of animals for their suggestions for a birthday present he plans to give his mother.

Freeman, Don (1968). *Corduroy*. New York: Viking Penguin.
A teddy bear's search for a lost button and a friend form the basis of this charming fantasy.

Green, John F. (1987). *There's a Dragon in My Closet*. Richmond Hill, Ontario: Scholastic.
What do you do when there's a dragon in your closet and nobody believes you? You invite your family and friends to

a dragon showing. But what happens when the dragon is frightened by so many visitors?

Hasely, Dennis (1987). *The Cave of Snores*. New York: Harper & Row.
Who or what could be making the strange sounds that emanate from a mysterious cave? Children are encouraged to suggest their own creative answers.

Hoban, Russell (1964). *Bread and Jam for Frances*. New York: Harper & Row.
Frances refuses to eat anything but bread and jam. This story recounts why he made that decision, and what happens.

Hobbs, Christopher (1990). *Jeremy and the Puddle*. Winchester, Massachusetts: Faber & Faber.
When a perfect puddle appears on Jeremy's street, he cannot resist jumping into it. His return from the strange world he encounters at the bottom depends on his knowledge of four magic words.

Hutchins, Hazel (1988). *The Three and Many Wishes of Jason Reid*. New York: Viking Penguin.
Jason, who loves reading fairy tales, is granted three magic wishes. Aware of the consequences of foolish requests, he works hard at following correct procedures. A funny and suspenseful tale perfect for a storytelling session.

Hutchins, Pat (1986). *The Doorbell Rang*. New York: Greenwillow.
Grandma bakes the best cookies, but when the doorbell rings repeatedly, will she have enough for all her guests? Humor and a surprise ending combine to present a charming tale.

Keller, H. (1990). *Henry's Happy Birthday*. New York: Greenwillow.
At Henry's birthday celebration everything goes wrong, including his choice of cake.

Kovalski, Maryann (1987). *The Wheels On The Bus*. Toronto: Kids Can Press.
A grandmother shares with her two grand-daughters a traditional song that she enjoyed as a child. The children enthusiastically join in the repetitive refrain.

Littledale, Freya (1969). *The Magic Fish*. New York: Scholastic.

A fisherman catches a magic fish that grants him one wish. The man offers the wish to his wife, and trouble follows when she keeps sending him back to demand another wish. Because of the memorable poem the man must say in order to call the fish, this story is particularly good for dramatization.

Lobel, Arnold (1985). *Whiskers and Rhymes*. New York: Greenwillow.
A lyrical selection of traditional and contemporary poems told in four lines of verse. A good example of how, through only a few imaginative words, an author can evoke emotions and images.

Mayer, Mercer (1976). *Liza Lou And The Yeller Belly Swamp*. New York: Macmillan.
In this tale, a little girl outwits a monster while crossing the swamp on the way to her grandmother's house.

Morgan, Allen (1984). *Matthew and the Midnight Tow Truck*. Toronto: Annick Press.
A little boy's love of tow trucks leads him on a midnight adventure in this fantasy tale.

Muller, Robin (1984). *Tatterhood*. Richmond Hill, Ontario: Scholastic.
This is an Irish version of Cinderella and makes an excellent choice for retelling.

Munsch, Robert (1985). *Mortimer*. Toronto: Annick.
A gifted storyteller, Robert Munsch has many excellent titles useful for the beginning storyteller, including *Love You Forever* (1986). In this one, a young boy's family have problems getting him to go to sleep. Children love to chime in with Mortimer's sleepytime noise and with the reactions of his family.

_____ (1980). *The Paperbag Princess*. Toronto: Annick.
When her friend is stolen by a dragon, Princess Elizabeth must fly around the world to save him. But what does the prince do instead of saying thank you? And how does Elizabeth respond? The unexpected answers will delight young and old listeners.

Murphy, Jill (1986). *Five Minutes' Peace*. New York: Putnam.
The importance of private family time, particularly for mother, is highlighted in this charming animal fantasy.

Numeroff, Laura J. (1985). *If You Give A Mouse A Cookie*. New York: Harper and Row.
> A little boy offers a hungry mouse a cookie and then spends all his time meeting the additional requests of the demanding creature.

Pearson, Susan (1987). *Happy Birthday Grampie*. New York: Dial.
> A grandparent's birthday is celebrated in a special way by an imaginative grandchild. The story depicts a loving relationship between two generations.

Porter, Sue (1989). *One Potato*. New York: Bradbury Press.
> The farm animals gather for a meal, but when only one potato is left, a contest begins to see who gets it. Children will delight in the surprise ending.

Prelutsky, Jack (1990). *Something Big Has Been Here*. New York: Greenwillow.
> Playful language and limited suspense combine to create a delightful collection of poems for children. The material, chosen for its child appeal, incorporates lyrical, narrative and humorous verses.

Sendak, Maurice (1963). *Where the Wild Things Are*. New York: Harper & Row.
> Like many of Sendak's other books, this title will delight young listeners.

Steig, William (1982). *Doctor Desoto*. New York: Farrar, Straus & Giroux.
> A mouse who is also a dentist is asked to care for a fox with a bad tooth. How the good doctor manages his work without being eaten will delight young listeners.

_____ (1969). *Sylvester and the Magic Pebble*. New York: Simon & Schuster.
> The police are called in to find Sylvester, who has been turned into stone by some misapplied magic.

Stevens, Carla (1982). *Anna, Grandpa, and the Big Storm*. Boston: Houghton Mifflin.
> The Great American Blizzard of 1888 is weathered by a courageous little girl and her wise grandfather.

Stevenson, James (1977). *Could Be Worse!* New York: Greenwillow.

Things may seem bad, but they could always be worse. For another story along this theme, see *It Could Always Be Worse* (New York: Farrar, Straus & Giroux, 1990) in the Jewish collection of Appendix D, page 60.

_____ (1983). *What's Under My Bed?* New York: Greenwillow. Grandpa spins tall tales in order to quell the nightly concerns of his grandchildren who fantasize about what is under their beds.

Williams, Linda (1986). *The Little Old Lady Who Was Not Afraid Of Anything*. New York: Harper & Row.
A courageous little old lady confronts a pumpkin head, a tall black hat, and many other spooky objects that follow her home on a dark night. The author has retold a traditional seasonal favorite for contemporary listeners.

Yashima, Taro (1976). *Crow Boy*. New York: Penguin.
The silent gifts of a shy school boy go unnoticed until a perceptive teacher brings them to the attention of his classmates and villagers.

Yolen, Jane (1974). *The Girl Who Cried Flowers and Other Tales*. New York: Harper & Row.
The power of kindness and the conquest of fear are dominant themes in this collection of five modern fairy tales. The settings of the stories are found 'on the far side of yesterday'. Their conversational style makes them a perfect choice for a storytelling session.

_____ (1978). *No Bath Tonight*. New York: Harper & Row.
Because of minor injuries, Jeremy avoids taking a nightly bath until Grandma uses her ingenuity on a Sunday evening.

Zemach, Margot (1976). *Hush Little Baby*. New York: Dutton.
How do you get a young baby to sleep? This book has a suggestion.

Zion, Gene (1976). *Harry The Dirty Dog*. New York: Harper & Row.
Harry's aversion to soap and water leads to non-acceptance by his family until his true identity is revealed.

Read-Alouds for Young Children

Aesop. See Clark, Margaret.
See Rackham, Arthur.

Allen, Pamela (1984). *Bertie and the Bear*. New York: Putnam.
A queen, a king and various other characters come to Bertie's rescue when he and a bear have an adventure.

Barrie, James (1904). *Peter Pan*. London: Penguin.
This is the original story of a little boy who finds himself in a fantasy land. Students might find it interesting to compare the original with the Walt Disney version. Also consider studying how Peter Pan changes throughout the series.

Baum, L. Frank (1904). *Land of Oz*. New York: Macmillan.
This is the original story of Dorothy's trip to Oz. While younger students will be delighted by the tale, older students may wish to compare the written and movie versions. What changes were made? Why?

Belpre, Pura (1978). *The Rainbow-Colored Horse*. New York: Warne.
An interesting tale about a horse of a rather unique color.

Blades, Ann (1971). *Mary of Mile 18*. Montreal: Tundra.
A wish on the Northern Lights makes a dream come true for a little girl who longs to adopt a homeless wolf pup.

Bond, Michael (1958). *A Bear Called Paddington*. London: Collins.
This is one of a series of delightful stories about Paddington Bear, a teddy bear who delights young children.

Briggs, Raymond (1970). *Jim and the Beanstalk*. New York: Coward.
This is a contemporary version of 'Jack and the Beanstalk' that will delight young listeners.

Bulla, Clyde R. (1990). *My Friend the Monster*. New York: Harper & Row.
The theme of friendship between two unlikely characters is explored in this delightful tale. As the story concludes, the author provides many opportunities to discuss what makes a good friend.

Clarke, Margaret (1990). *The Best of Aesop's Fables*. Boston: Little, Brown.

The most popular of the wise beast/foolish beast tales have been chosen for this collection of fables. Children will laugh at the foolishness and admire the wisdom of various animal characters.

Climo, Shirley (1988). *King of the Birds*. New York: Harper & Row.

A search for a king of all birds takes an unexpected twist in this story based on one of the world's oldest legends.

Cole, William (1978). *Oh, Such Foolishness!* New York: Harper & Row.

As his titles suggest, Cole uses words in ways that delight young listeners.

Dahl, Roald (1964). *Charlie & the Chocolate Factory*. New York: Knopf.

This story of greed and avarice continues to delight young listeners.

de Paola, Tomie (1990). *Tomie de Paola's Book of Bible Stories*. New York: Putnam.

From a literary perspective, the Bible contains myths, legends, fables, parables and proverbs to share with children. This author/illustrator presents his personal favorites in a way that is reflective of the oral tradition of many of the stories.

Denton, Kady M. (1988). *Granny Is A Darling*. New York: Macmillan.

When a loving Granny comes to spend the night, her young grandson must protect her from the scary things he imagines are found in the dark.

Dewey, Ariane (1988). *The Tea Squall*. New York: Greenwillow.

Tall-tale heroines try to outdo each other in their exaggerated stories shared around a tea table. Imaginative use of language is evident in the outrageous tales.

Gag, Wanda (1928). *Millions of Cats*. New York: Coward.

When an old man goes to find his wife a new pet, millions of cats want to go home with him. But how can he and his wife care for so many? The solution delights young listeners.

Gilman, Phoebe (1984). *The Balloon Tree*. Richmond Hill, Ontario: North Winds Press.

When Princess Leora's father has to go away, the Archduke is left in charge. What happens when the Archduke breaks all the balloons Princess Leora uses to contact her father when she's in trouble? The conclusion to this tale will amaze and amuse young audiences.

Herriot, James (1990). *Oscar-Cat-About Town* London: St. Martin's Press.
One of the excellent stories told by James Herriot, who uses humor and nostalgia in talking about some of the experiences he had as a veterinarian.

Hines, A. (1990). *The Secret Keeper*. New York: Greenwillow.
Some secrets are hard to keep, but Josh has a very important one. When Grandmother arrives at Christmastime, the special secret is shared.

Kellogg, Steven (1985). *Chicken Little*. New York: William Morrow.
This is an off-beat and updated version of the usual 'Chicken Little' story that can be used to motivate students to write their own modern versions of favorite fairy tales.

Kipling, Rudyard (1902). *Just So Stories*. London: Macmillan.
Creative explanations as to how certain animals received their distinctive characteristics are shared by a gifted author. Because Kipling's style is so rich in the sounds of language, his work requires an exact reading of his prose.

_____ (1894). *The Jungle Book*. London: Macmillan.
This is the first well-known children's book written by Rudyard Kipling, and one that continues to be popular. If possible, try to get one of the original versions rather than a Walt Disney edition.

Little, Jean (1985). *Lost and Found*. Toronto: Viking Kestrel Canada.
Finding a runaway dog in her neighborhood eases the loneliness Lucy feels at losing her old friends. The search for the dog's owner, however, creates problems that she did not expect.

Lobel, Arnold (1981). *Uncle Elephant*. New York: Harper & Row.
A nephew whose parents are missing at sea is entertained by Uncle Elephant's wondrous tales. Fortunately, as the narrator

is about to run out of stories, the parents return home to tell of their own marvellous adventures.

Lofting, Hugh (1920). *The Voyage of Doctor Dolittle*. London: Cape.
This is the story of a doctor who learns to talk to animals, and of the many animals who dominate his home and surgery. Because of its popularity, it developed into a series.

Lunn, Janet (1989). *Duck Cakes For Sale*. Toronto: Groundwood/Douglas & McIntyre.
A little old woman's move from the city to the country results in an enterprising business when she begins to care for ducklings on her small farm. This cumulative tale with its humorous repetitions will delight young listeners.

Mahy, Margaret (1983). *The Boy Who Was Followed Home*. New York: Dial.
Robert is followed home by some friendly hippos. The way he persuades the uninvited guests to leave is a good example of problem solving.

McCloskey, Robert (1948). *Blueberries for Sal*. New York: Viking Penguin.
A small child and her mother go blueberrying. The story tells about how they pick and can their produce, and of what happens when they meet a mother bear who wants to pick blueberries for her young one.

McNicoll, Sylvia (1990). *Project Disaster*. Richmond Hill, Ontario: Scholastic Canada.
Neil's goldfish dies, and he desperately searches for a replacement Science Fair experiment. When everything he tries turns into a disaster, Neil hopes to forget his shame by taking his grandfather's car for a spin — only he can't drive.

Milne, A. A. (1926). *Winnie The Pooh*. London: Methuen.
Christopher Robin's animal toys come to life in these whimsical tales of childhood. The author's skilfully crafted language embodies comforting themes that make the stories ideal for a read-aloud session.

Moore, Lilian (1988). *I'll Meet You At The Cucumbers*. New York: Macmillan.
A little country mouse conquers his fear of the unknown as he visits a major city. The author gives a gentle poetic treat-

ment to her message of making the most of one's talents and opportunities.

Noble, Trinka H. (1980). *The Day Jimmy's Boa Ate The Wash*. New York: Dial.
When a boy drops his pet boa in the hen house, unplanned havoc results. Another title to encourage prediction is the sequel: *Jimmy's Boa Bounces Back*, Dial, 1984.

Numeroff, Laura J. (1985). *If You Give A Mouse A Cookie*. New York: Harper & Row.
Be prepared for some hilarious consequences if you give a mouse a cookie. Children can extend the mouse motif or choose another creature for their own main protagonists.

Parish, Peggy (1963). *Amelia Bedelia*. New York: Harper & Row.
Amelia Bedelia has a hard time understanding the directions of her new boss. Fortunately, she saves the day when she bakes the best lemon meringue pie in the world. This and the other Amelia Bedelia books will help children understand that people do not always say what they mean — or understand what they hear.

Potter, Beatrix (1904). *The Tale of Benjamin Bunny*. London: Frederick Warne.
Beatrix Potter's stories with their almost human animals, challenging vocabulary, and beautiful watercolors have fascinated generations of children. While some stories may seem a little dated, they still interest young readers.

_____ (1906). *The Tale of Peter Rabbit*. London: Frederick Warne.
Peter Rabbit, with his disobedient ways, is a character that has delighted generations of children.

Rackham, Arthur (1931). *Aesop's Fables*. London: Heinemann.
This is a traditional retelling of the stories about smart/foolish animals. A useful American version is that by L. Untermeyer, New York: Golden, 1965. Unfortunately, the Untermeyer edition is currently out of print and therefore confined to libraries.

Scieszka, Jan (1989). *The True Story of the Three Little Pigs*. New York: Viking Penguin.
This contemporary version of an old favorite will delight youngsters.

Schwartz, Amy (1983). *Bea and Mr. Jones*. New York: Bradbury Press.

A humorous solution to the tedium of a daily schedule results when Bea, a kindergartner, and her father, an advertising executive, change places.

Seuss, Dr. (1938). *The Five Hundred Hats of Bartholomew Cubbins*. New York: Random House.

Bartholomew has so many hats he can't remove them all, even when it's a choice between that and death. What will happen?

Siamon, Sharon (1987). *Fishing for Trouble*. Toronto: Lorimer.

Until Remington Wickers arrives in the 'Salmon Snatcher', a boat equipped with all the most modern fish-finding gadgets, Kiff Kokatow plans to win the Big Pickle Lake Fish Derby. How can he beat Remington, especially when his best plans are foiled by Josie Moon, who also wants to win that derby? The solution is simple — and entertaining.

Thiele, Colin (1988). *Farmer Schulz's Ducks*. New York: Harper & Row.

An Australian farm near a busy highway is the home for fifty ducks with ''necks of opal and wings of amethyst.'' The creatures are threatened by impatient drivers until a little girl finds a creative solution to their problem.

Tresselt, Alvin R. (1947). *White Snow, Bright Snow*. New York: Lothrop, Lee & Shepard Books.

The similes in this book help children to see their world in a new and imaginative way.

Tulloch, Richard (1987). *Stories From Our House*. Cambridge: Cambridge.

A delightful family in a disorganized household shares its daily life with young listeners. An invasion of ants, spilt milk and a host of other minor problems present a realistic setting for children.

Viorst, Judith (1972). *Alexander and the Terrible, Horrible, No Good, Very Bad Day*. New York: Macmillan.

A little boy's day goes from bad to worse, but a sympathetic mother makes him realize that everyone has days just like his.

Wallace, Ian (1986). *The Sparrow's Song*. Toronto: Penguin.

A younger brother and sister raise an orphaned sparrow to maturity then, with conflicting emotions, set it free.

Waterton, Betty (1980). *Pettranella*. Vancouver, British Columbia: Douglas & McIntyre.
A young immigrant to Canada loses her grandmother's precious gift of flower seeds. In the spring, they are discovered as colorful, flourishing plants symbolic of Pettranella's new life.

Waters, Kate and Madeline Slovenz-Low (1990). *Lion Dancer: Ernie Wan's Chinese New Year*. New York: Scholastic.
Six-year-old Ernie Wan prepares for his first Chinese New Year's parade as a lion dancer. The importance of this event provides an educational perspective for children.

Wells, Rosemary (1973). *Noisy Nora*. New York: Dial.
The middle child in a mouse family uses boisterous activities to try to gain her family's attention. Through the author's use of humor, children see a view of life that makes it easier to accept misfortunes and disappointments.

Willis, Val (1990). *The Surprise in the Wardrobe*. New York: Farrar, Straus & Giroux.
A closet may hold many strange items but the most mysterious of all is discovered one magic day. The sequential plot encourages children to make their own predictions about the surprise.

Wilson, Budge (1984). *The Worst Christmas Present Ever*. Richmond Hill, Ontario: Scholastic.
Ten-year-old Lorinda thinks she has found the perfect Christmas present for her mother. Now all she has to do is earn enough money to buy it. After all that trouble, what should Lorinda do when she learns her mother's real opinion of the gift she has worked so long to purchase? Readers interested in Lorinda's determined ways may be interested in two other books about her: *A House Far From Home* (1986) and *Mystery Lights At Blue Harbour* (1987).

Yolen, Jane (1990). *The Dragon's Boy*. New York: Harper & Row.
A kindly dragon helps a homeless boy face his destiny of becoming a king. The author is noted for her contemporary fairy tales and legends.

Alexander, Lloyd (1984). *The Beggar Queen*. New York: Dutton.
The story of the beggar maid Mickle begun in the book *Westmark* (Dutton, 1981), and continued through *The Kestrel* (Dutton, 1982), concludes with this final novel in the trilogy. High adventure is paralleled with strong characterizations and a tightly written style.

_____ (1968). *The High King*. New York: Henry Holt.
This is the fifth and concluding volume in the saga of Taran, the assistant pig-keeper who finds his real heritage.

Bradford, Karleen (1989). *Windward Island*. Toronto: Kids Can Press.
When the government automates all the lighthouses, Loren knows that he and his father must leave Windward Island. He and his best friend, Caleb, plan to spend a last carefree summer together until the unexpected arrival of April, a teenager who has just lost her mother, causes a rift between them. The story of how Loren learns to accept change will interest older students who are having to cope with their own problems around maturing.

Brittain, Bill (1983). *The Wish Giver: Three Tales of Coven Tree*. New York: Harper & Row.
A mysterious stranger who promises wishes-to-come-true for fifty cents creates mystery and suspense for three young recipients.

Burnford, Sheila (1960). *The Incredible Journey*. Boston: Little, Brown.
This is the story of two dogs and a cat who make their way across an isolated section of Northern Ontario in search of their owner.

Cleary, Beverley (1955). *Beezus and Ramona*. New York: William Morrow.
Young children are fascinated by the antics of Ramona in this and any of the other numerous books about the same character.

de Angeli, Marguerite (1949). *The Door in the Wall: Story of Medieval London*. New York: Doubleday.
Set in the Middle Ages, the trials and successes of a lame

castle page make for an entertaining story. Robin saves the castle from a marauding army and receives royal recognition for his bravery. The story depicts the pageantry and color of an exciting historical period.

Godfrey, Martin (1990). *Can You Teach Me To Pick My Nose?* New York: Avon.
What student doesn't want to be part of the 'in' crowd? To be accepted by the grade sevens in his new school, Jordy feels he has to impress his peers, an aim that includes claiming that he was the skateboard champion in his home town. Despite his desire to be accepted, Jordy finally recognizes real friendship when it is offered to him.

Griffith, Helen (1990). *Caitlin's Holiday.* New York: Greenwillow.
A doll named Holiday who can walk and speak proves to be an unusual companion for Caitlin. The appeal of an inanimate object coming to life is the basis for this suspenseful fantasy.

Halvorson, Marilyn (1988). *Dare.* Toronto: Stoddart.
When their grandmother dies, Dare (almost 16) and his 12-year-old brother Ty must choose between a foster home and living with Laura McConnell, a part-time teacher. Although Ty loves Laura, Dare and she are in constant conflict, especially after he kills Laura's favorite horse. But then, Dare is afraid to get close to people. To do so would mean facing a past that is too painful to remember.

Henry, Marguerite (1947). *Misty of Chincoteague.* New York: Macmillan.
A wild pony who loves her freedom and two children who befriend her have many adventures on two islands off the shores of Virginia. Another favorite by the same author is *King of the Wind* (1948), a fictional story about a real stallion and his friendship with a mute stable boy.

Hughes, Ted (1988). *The Iron Giant: A Story in Five Nights.* New York: Harper & Row.
A seemingly invincible giant robot without a master emerges from the sea and stalks the land. The boy, Hogarth, befriends the iron man who finds that he must fight for his life when alien creatures attack the earth. As the subtitle suggests, this suspenseful story is perfect for five separate read-aloud sessions.

Laurence, Margaret (1979). *The Olden Days Coat*. Toronto: McClelland & Stewart.

An old winter coat transports Sal back to a long ago Christmas where she encounters her grandmother as a little girl. This time travel fantasy highlights the empathy between several generations.

Lewis, C. S. (1950). *The Lion, The Witch, and The Wardrobe*. London: Collins.

The back of a wardrobe leads to a land called Narnia, where it always snows but is never Christmas. Peter, Susan, Edmund, and Lucy must help break the wicked Snow Queen's magic spell. An outstanding example of high fantasy for children.

Lowry, Lois (1986). *Anastasia On Her Own*. Boston: Houghton Mifflin.

A mother's business trip gives Anastasia the opportunity to put her household organizational skills to work. She discovers that caring for a house is much easier than it looks.

Mahy, Margaret (1981). *The Great Piratical Rumbustification* and *The Librarian and the Robbers*. London: Penguin.

These two short novels by an excellent New Zealand storyteller provide laughter for listeners of all ages. The first story in the volume recounts the tale of a band of retired pirates who, because they dislike inactivity, respond to a babysitting advertisement. Their plan is to hold a reunion of their former mates during a giant pirate party. In the second, a group of non-reading robbers take a librarian hostage. A devotee of reading aloud, she turns her captors into voracious readers.

Martel, Suzanne (1985). *Robot Alert*. Toronto: Kids Can Press.

When Eve Kevin and Adam Colbert receive gift robots, they discover that their toys are really aliens sent from another planet to help save Earth from destruction. The children gain in confidence as they play a vital role in the robots' secret mission.

McCloskey, Robert (1943). *Homer Price*. New York: Viking Penguin.

Homer is a little boy who gets into some ridiculous situations in a small town that appears ordinary.

Miles, Bernard (1979). *Robin Hood: His Life and Legend*. New York: Macmillan.

Exiled from his vast estate, the man who was to become known as Robin Hood takes refuge in Sherwood Forest. With his band of Merry Men, he fights against the Sheriff of Nottingham's tyranny and assists the poor. Encourage students to compare these characters with those portrayed in the modern movie.

Paterson, Katherine (1977). *Bridge to Terabithia*. New York: Harper & Row.

Two nonconformists develop a firm friendship. Between them, they invent a fantasy kingdom named Terabithia. Tragedy ensues when one of the characters loses her life while attempting to get across to Terabithia. The survivor struggles with his feelings about the loss and eventually gains a greater appreciation of life.

————, (1978). *The Great Gilly Hopkins*. New York: Crowell.

Until Gilly experiences the unquestioning love of Mame Trotter, she is determined to be so bad that no foster home will keep her. Too bad she had already written a letter describing Trotter's home in most uncomplimentary terms, and begging to be removed.

Pearson, Kit (1987). *A Handful of Time*. Markham, Ontario: Penguin Books Canada.

An old watch hidden under a floorboard becomes the catalyst to take Patricia back to another era. In her travels between the past and the present, she discovers the mystery surrounding the timepiece and also that of her troubled family.

Rosenberg, Jane (1985). *Dance Me A Story: Twelve Tales from the Classic Ballets*. New York: Thames & Hudson.

Twelve classic ballets are retold as fairy tales for young listeners. The expressive movement of the dance is revealed through the imaginative style of the author.

Schlein, Miriam (1990). *The Year of the Panda*. New York: Harper & Row.

Fearing for the safety of an orphaned Panda, Lu Yi makes a dangerous journey in order to bring the young animal to the Panda Rescue Center in Asia.

Scholes, Katherine (1989). *The Landing: A Night of Birds*. New York: Doubleday.

Annie and her grandfather, a boat builder, live by the sea. During a violent storm, the two risk their lives to rescue a flock of struggling birds.

Story, Alice (1989). *Beneath the Barrens*. St. John's, Newfoundland: Breakwater Books.
Kate and her companion, Frazer, an independent cat, encounter subterranean adventure when they meet a number of miniature creatures who live under Newfoundland's rocks and bracken.

Thiele, Colin (1988). *Shadow Shark*. New York: Harper & Row.
Young Joe is sent to a tiny Australian town to live with relatives. Feeling unwanted and misunderstood, he makes friends with a stray dog. Together they experience high adventure during a hunt for a white shark.

Truss, Jan (1982). *Jasmin*. Vancouver: Douglas & McIntyre.
Although Jasmin wants to do well at school, her large family makes it impossible for her to do homework. Feeling alone and misunderstood, Jasmin runs away to the wilderness, where she meets a couple who help her change her life.

White, E. B. (1952). *Charlotte's Web*. New York: Harper & Row.
This is the popular tale of Charlotte, an ingenious spider who saves her favorite pig from the slaughterhouse. Charlotte's conversations with the pig and her philosophy fascinate most young and old readers.

Wilson, Budge (1988). *Breakdown*. Richmond Hill, Ontario: Scholastic.
When their father has a nervous breakdown, 13-year-old Katie and her younger brother, Daniel, notice a lot of changes. At first, the changes are bad. As their father gets better, however, they begin to see some positive results of his illness. This is a thoughtful book that will help students understand mental illness.

Winthrop, Elizabeth (1986). *The Castle in the Attic*. New York: Bantam.
A time travel device in the form of a wooden model castle transports William back to medieval times for exciting adventures.

Yep, Laurence (1977). *Child of the Owl*. New York: Harper & Row. San Francisco is the setting for this story about a young girl who learns to appreciate her heritage.

. . . .

APPENDIX D

Stories from Around the World

Most experts in the field of storytelling recommend folk literature as a starting point for the beginning storyteller. Children
who have listened to the folklore of many cultures begin to see
recurring themes as people's beliefs, dreams, hopes, fears and
values are shared through their traditional literature. By know-
ing about these stories, and by sharing them with children,
storytellers help to build bridges of understanding.

The following list of stories may prove successful in introducing other cultures in a positive way. Several of the titles, sad
to say, are no longer in print, but that does not mean that they
have vanished off the face of the earth! They will still be available in libraries and private collections, and if you can't find the
edition I recommend then the librarian or bookseller will certainly be able to suggest a substitute.

I have recommended the particular edition of the story which
I have most enjoyed using as a storyteller in North America. This
choice was simply based on my own successful experience with
that edition; you may well know and love other editions of the
same title, of which I am unfortunately unaware, one of which
is available in your country but not in mine. My list, then, is
a personal one, as will be yours. Each of us would enjoy know-
ing of and sharing each other's lists. My list of stories from
around the world is divided into the following categories:

General Collections
Africa
Asia
Caribbean
Europe (Central)

India
Jewish Culture
Mediterranean
Middle East
North America (including Mexico)
Russia
Scandinavia
South America
South Pacific (Australia and New Zealand)
United Kingdom

GENERAL COLLECTIONS

Clarkson, Atelia and Gilbert B. Cross, ed. (1982). *World Folktales*. New York: Macmillan.
This excellent resource collection includes a number of genres such as formula tales and trickster tales, as well as information on how to use such stories in elementary and college classrooms.

Cole, Joanna, ed. (1983). *Best Loved Folktales of the World*. New York: Doubleday.
Humor and romance highlight the favorite everyday folk tales of the world's people in this splendid classroom collection. Includes useful indexes.

Crouch, M. (1983). *The Whole World Storybook*. New York: Oxford.
Currently out of print, this book outlines twenty-five stories from Korea, Portugal, Greece and Hungary, that are suitable for five- to 10-year-old children. Look for it in a research library.

de Paola, Tomie (1986). *Tomie de Paola's Favorite Nursery Tales*. New York: Putnam.
This richly illustrated classic includes thirty well-known nursery tales.

Hamilton, Virginia (1985). *Favorite Fairy Tales Told Around The World*. Boston: Little, Brown.
This is a wide ranging collection of tales from many nations that will interest both the beginning and more experienced storyteller.

Lurie, Alison (1980). *Clever Gretchen and Other Forgotten Folktales*. New York: Harper & Row.
This collection includes fifteen tales about girls who are clever,

active, witty, and resourceful. Gretchen, for example, disguises herself as a bird to fool the devil.

Minard, Rosemary ed. (1975). *Womenfolk and Fairy Tales*. Boston: Houghton Mifflin.
Eighteen traditional tales highlight female protagonists who are decisive in determining their adventures and fates. The contents include the stories of Molly Whuppie, Clever Elsie, and Three Strong Women. How are females portrayed in fairy tales? This book offers a full and satisfying answer to that question.

Pellowski, Anne (1984). *The Story Vine: A Source Book of Unusual and Easy-To-Tell Stories from Around the World*. New York: Macmillan.
The author has collected and recommends a list of simple narratives gathered from the world's resources for children. An international authority on storytelling, Pellowski suggests that the tales be accompanied by string figures (South Pacific stories), nesting dolls (Russian stories), sand paintings (Australian myths), and story vines (African folklore). A list of Pellowski's personal favorites is included.

Yolen, Jane, ed. (1986). *Favorite Folktales From Around the World*. New York: Pantheon.
Edited by Jane Yolen, herself an excellent storyteller, this volume contains fairy tales from many countries.

AFRICA

Aardema, Verna (1985). *Bimwilli and the Zimwi*. New York: Dial.
Aardema retells a popular tale from Tanzania and Zanzibar.

_____ (1981). *Bringing The Rain To Kapiti Plain*. New York: Dial.
An African cumulative tale is told in lilting rhyme. A repetitive refrain describes the drought conditions on the land until a welcome rain cloud appears.

_____ (1984). *Oh, Kojo! How Could You!* New York: Dial.
A renowned storyteller retells this West African tale in a way that will attract young audiences.

_____ (1960). *Tales From The Story Hat: African Folktales*. New York: Coward.
Although this book is unfortunately out of print, it is important because it emphasizes the importance of passing on oral

tales. Since copies are available in some larger libraries, try to get a copy through inter-library loan.

_____ (1978). *Why Mosquitoes Buzz in People's Ears: A West African Tale*. New York: Dial.
This West African 'pourquoi' tale relates why mosquitoes buzz as they do.

Ashley, Bryan (1986). *Beat the Story-Drum, Pum-Pum*. New York: Macmillan.
This book recounts five Nigerian tales, including why frog and snake, who were good friends, no longer play together; and the story of the husband who couldn't stay married because he counted every spoonful his wife served.

_____ (1985). *The Cat's Purr*. New York: Macmillan.
This is a story from the Antilles about rat and cat, who were the best of friends, until a drum passed down in cat's family caused a separation. Cat finally swallowed the drum, which still begins to beat whenever a cat is gently stroked.

Courlander, Harold and George Herzog (1988). *The Cow Tail Switch and Other West African Stories*. New York: Henry Holt.
The title story in this 17-story volume is a resurrection myth about a man who is not dead because he isn't forgotten by his youngest son.

Courlander, Harold. *The Crest and the Hide: Other African Stories*. New York: Putnam.
This book offers several stories that can be used to motivate students to use folklore techniques in their own storytelling and writing.

Grifalconi, Ann (1986). *Village of Round and Square Houses*. Boston: Little, Brown.
In a village in the hills of Cameroon, in central Africa, the women live in round houses, the men in square ones. This tales tells why they do this, and how it has brought peace to the community.

Haley, Gail E. (1970) *A Story, A Story*. New York: Macmillan.
Long ago, there were no stories. Then Kwaka Ananse, or spider man, spun a web up to the sky to bargain with the sky god for stories. This traditional tale tells how the bargain was struck and paid for.

McDermott, Gerald (1972). *Anansi The Spider: A Tale from the Ashanti*. New York: Henry Holt.

This West African folk tale explains what spider weaves into his six sons.

Pitcher, Diana (1981). *Tokolishi: African Folk Tales Retold*. Berkeley, California: Celestial Arts Publishing Co.

These African tales from Bantu sources are told in a lively style incorporating the rhythm and cadence of narratives shared from an oral tradition.

Rose, A. (1982). *Pot Full of Luck*. New York: Lothrop, Lee and Shepard Books.

When Mumba gets tired of all the villagers who come to him for advice, he asks his wife to make a clay pot in which he can store his wits. But what happens when the pot breaks! This African pattern tale will appeal to the imagination of many children. Although it is out of print, it is available in some libraries.

Steptoe, John (1987). *Mufaro's Beautiful Daughters: An African Tale*. New York: Lothrop, Lee and Shepard Books.

This African 'pourquoi' tale is the story of two sisters. One is kind, the other selfish. When the king begins looking for a wife, both daughters try their luck.

ASIA

A.-Ling, Louis (1982). *Yeh-Shen: A Cinderella Story From China*. New York: Putnam.

Cinderella fans will be interested in this Chinese tale of a young daughter who is raised by her father's second wife. Left behind at festival time, the girl cries over the bones of a fish which she had raised and her stepmother had killed. The fish helps her dress for the festival. As she is leaving the celebration, however, the girl loses a shoe. When the king sees how tiny it is, he is obsessed with the desire to meet the owner.

Asian Cultural Center for UNESCO (1977). *Folk Tales From Asia For Children Everywhere*. Book Five. New York: Weatherhill.

This volume retells stories from Burma, Iran, Japan, Malaysia, Pakistan, and the Philippines.

Clark, A. (1979). *In the Land of Small Dragon*. New York: Viking.

In this Vietnamese version of the Cinderella story told in verse, a bird drops a young girl's 'hai' (slipper) in front of the emperor as he walks in the garden. The book is out of print but available in some libraries, and of interest to those intrigued by the many forms Cinderella can take.

Haviland, V. (1967). *Favorite Fairy Tales Told in Japan*. Boston: Little, Brown.
This book tells five Japanese fairy tales, including 'The Good Fortune Kettle', the story of a badger who turns into a tea kettle to reward the person who set him free from a trap. Because of their unique Japanese flavor, these tales are well worth the search in a library specializing in folklore to find this out-of-print volume.

Heyer, Marilee (1986). *The Weaving of a Dream: A Chinese Folktale*. New York: Viking Penguin.
This is a delicately told Chinese folk tale that will interest young listeners.

Hughes, Monica (1989). *Little Fingerling*. Toronto: Kids Can Press.
This Japanese folk tale is about a tiny boy who has the heart of a giant. For another retelling of the same story, see *The Inch Boy* by Junko Marimoto.

Laurin, Anne (1981). *The Perfect Crane*. New York: Harper & Row.
This is the interpretation of a popular Japanese folk tale. The original tale is about a crane who made herself into a woman to thank a kind farmer for saving her life. Also see *The Crane Wife* by Sumiko Yagawa.

Lee, Jeanne M. (1985). *Toad is the Uncle of Heaven: A Vietnamese Folk Tale*. New York: Henry Holt.
Listeners interested in Asian folk tales will be fascinated by this story from Vietnam.

Marimoto, Junko (1988). *The Inch Boy*. New York: Penguin.
This Japanese version of 'Tom Thumb' is about a tiny boy who goes to the capital to work in a palace. His job is to hold the princess's papers as she reads. The pair fall in love, and when the tiny boy saves the princess from a dragon, he gives her the one wish he has been granted.

Newton, P. (1982). *The Five Sparrows*. New York: Atheneum.
A sparrow who has been nursed by a Japanese woman presents her with a seed that produces magic gourds. Although this

book is currently out of print, it is available at some libraries that specialize in children's literature.

Philip, N., ed (1986). *The Spring of Butterflies and Other Folktales of China's Minority Peoples*. New York: Lothrop, Lee and Shepard Books.
　The title story tells of a girl whose head is so turned by spring that she disobeys her elders but is saved by love. Because this particular tale is unique to Asian countries, and illustrates an important aspect of Chinese culture (reverence for elders), it is well worth the search in a large reference library that carries books which are currently out of print.

Seros, Kathleen (1982). *Sun and Moon: Fairy Tales From Korea*. Elizabeth, New Jersey: Hollym International Corp.
　How did the sun and moon get into the sky? Perhaps they were a brother and sister who climbed into heaven to escape a tiger who had eaten their mother.

Vuong, Lynette D. (1982). *The Brocaded Slipper and Other Vietnamese Tales*. New York: Harper & Row.
　'The Brocaded Slipper' is the story of two sisters. The kind one receives help from a genie who gives her a little blue fish. When the fish is later killed by the cruel sister, it becomes a slipper which is carried by a crow to the king's palace.

Wallace, Ian (1984). *Chin Chiang and the Dragon's Dance*. Toronto: Groundwood/Douglas & McIntyre.
　Written and illustrated by Ian Wallace, this is the perceptive retelling of a traditional Chinese story in which a young boy is afraid he will disgrace both himself and his family because he doesn't know the dragon's dance.

Wolkstein, Diane (1983). *The Magic Wings: A Tale From China*. New York: E. P. Dutton.
　What happens when someone gets a pair of wings? This story offers a unique Chinese answer.

Yagawa, Sumiko (1981). *The Crane Wife*. New York: William Morrow.
　This is the Japanese story of a peasant who saves a crane from being killed. That night, a beautiful woman appears and begs him to marry her. She makes the man rich with her weaving until the man finds out the secret of her beautiful cloth.

Wolkstein, Diane (1978). *The Magic Orange Tree and Other Haitian Folktales*. New York: Knopf.

This collection of Haitian tales shows a mix of African and European cultures. The title story is about a tree that grows at the command of a child. Storytellers working in areas with a large Caribbean population will find this book particularly useful and worth the search through a reference section specializing in out-of-print volumes of folklore.

EUROPE

Carlson, N. (1980). *King of the Cats and Other Tales*. New York: Doubleday.

This book outlines eight legendary creatures of Breton folklore. The title story tells of a woman who befriends a kitten, and how, when he becomes the King of Cats, this kitten repays the dog who threatened him. Since children are fascinated by animals, particularly those with a mind of their own, storytellers will be glad they took the time to search for this volume, which is currently out of print. Try the reference section of a university library specializing in children's literature.

Crossley-Holland, Kevin (1986). *The Fox and the Cat: Animal Tales From Grimm*. New York: Lothrop, Lee and Shepard Books.

The fox is very proud of his craftiness. The cat humbly admits that all she can do is climb a tree. But when the dogs come to get him, fox wishes he knew how to climb, too. This, and other animal stories collected by the Grimm brothers, will entrance young listeners.

Domanska, Janina (1985). *Busy Monday Morning*. New York: Greenwillow.

A children's Polish folk song is the basis for this narrative incorporating the days of the week and the duties ascribed to them. The rhythm of the author's language encourages children to participate.

Galdone, Paul (1981). *The Amazing Pig: An Old Hungarian Tale*. Boston: Houghton Mifflin.

A king offers to give his daughter's hand to someone who tells him something that he can't believe. A peasant's son does.

Hort, Lenny (1987). *The Boy Who Held Back The Sea*. New York: Dial.

This is a retelling of the classic tale of the courageous Dutch boy who saves his village from a flood. Young listeners will revel in the exploits of this tiny hero.

Hutton, Warwick (1985). *Beauty and the Beast*. New York: Macmillan.

To save her father, a beautiful girl must live with an ugly monster. Through her love, however, she saves the monster, who turns out to be an enchanted prince. This is an interesting French version of the common European tale.

Langton, Jane (1985). *The Hedgehog Boy*. New York: Harper & Row.

This traditional Latvian tale will amuse young audiences.

Lewis, Naomi, ed. (1986). *The Twelve Dancing Princesses and Other Tales From Grimm*. New York: Dial.

Every morning the twelve princesses have to get new shoes because they have danced their old ones to pieces. Their father is desperate to know why. After others fail, a soldier succeeds in finding their secret and wins the hand of one of the girls.

Massignon, Genevieve (1978). *Folktales of France*. Ann Arbor, Michigan: Books on Demand.

This is an excellent collection of traditional French tales that will certainly please both storytellers and their audiences.

McGovern, Ann (1986). *Stone Soup*. New York: Scholastic.

After being refused food, a group of soldiers offer to make soup for some villagers. What goes well with stone soup? A bone, carrots, onions, etc. In the end, both the soldiers and the villagers are well fed. This is a French version of a popular European tale.

Rackham, Arthur (1920). *The Sleeping Beauty*. New York: Dover.

This is one of the earliest translations from the French of this popular fairy tale. For another interesting version, see the one by D. Walker, New York: Crowell.

Severo, E. (1981). *The Goodhearted Youngest Brother*. New York: Bradbury Press.

Three orphaned brothers must share two guns between them. The youngest brother volunteers to do without a gun, and later saves animals who help him solve the riddle of the bewitched princess. This Hungarian tale is not very well known, and therefore worth the trouble to find from a library which retains out-of-print volumes.

Tardi, Jacques (1984). *The Enchanted Pig: A Rumanian Fairy Tale.* Mankato, Minnesota: Creative Education, Inc.
An old couple who want a child are given an intelligent pig who grows up to earn a princess. When the princess burns the pig's skin, she loses her husband and must go to find him. In doing so, she releases the pig from its spell.

Tahjian, Virginia (1971). *Three Apples Fell From Heaven: Armenian Tales Retold.* Boston: Little, Brown.
Each of these tales ends with a touching line that encourages young listeners to develop their own concluding sentences: "One for the storyteller, one for the listener, and one for the one who truly hears ."

INDIA

Brown, M. (1977). *The Blue Jackal.* New York: Charles Scribner's Sons.
This story tells how the jackal becomes king of the animals under false pretences when he jumps into a vat of indigo to escape some dogs. He is later dethroned when his true color is discovered. Although out of print, this amusing tale is available from some libraries, and is usually a hit with young audiences.

Cowell, E. B., ed. (1981). *Jataka Stories.* Oxford: Pali Text Society.
Jataka tales are to Buddhist culture what Aesop is to Western culture. They point to the importance of the individual and the use of reality in solving life's problems. A more interesting, but out of print, version of these stories is *Jataka Tales* edited by N. De Roin, Boston: Houghton Mifflin, 1975.

Hitchcock, P. (1976). *The King Who Rides a Tiger and Other Folk Tales From Nepal.* Boston: Parnassus.
These twelve stories from the Himalayas include the tale of a poor farmer who helps a cobra. The cobra gives him a dog who turns into a beautiful girl in time to make his supper each night. The book is currently out of print; but since the magical tales will interest young readers, it's worth searching for in a large reference library.

Schwartz, Howard (1983). *Elijah's Violin and Other Jewish Fairy Tales*. New York: Harper & Row.

This is a selection of tales as retold by Howard Schwartz with an introduction by the author. The volume is out of print but available from some libraries. Libraries at Teachers' Colleges and other teacher training institutions often have good collections of traditional tales. Check with the closest institution.

Serwer-Bernstein, Blanche (1987). *Let's Steal the Moon*. New York: Shapolsky Publishers.

These are modern retellings of several ancient and more recent Jewish tales.

Shulevitz, Uri and I. L. Peretz (1985). *The Magician*. New York: Macmillan.

This is an adaptation from Yiddish of the story of the prophet Elijah, who disguises himself as a magician to visit the humblest homes during Passover. According to custom, one family is rewarded with a true Passover feast.

Singer, Isaac Bashevis (1982). *The Golem*. New York: Farrar, Straus and Giroux.

A clay giant who helps Jews in time of need is brought to life when the rabbi inscribes a name on its forehead. Through misuse, however, the rabbi loses control over the Golem. The Jewish race is threatened until a young servant girl saves the day but loses her heart.

Zemach, Margot G. (1990). *It Could Always Be Worse*. New York: Farrar, Straus & Giroux.

This is the story of a poor man who complains about his position in life. When his life changes, he quickly sees that things could be much worse, and learns to be happy with his lot.

MEDITERRANEAN

Basile, G. (1981). *Petrosinella: A Neopolitan Rapunzel*. New York: Frederick Warne.

This early version of 'Rapunzel' was popular in the Mediterranean at least 200 years before Grimm. In it, Petrosinella, which means parsley, learns that she is kept enchanted by three acorns in the rafters of her tower. When she takes the acorns with her, the witch chases both her and the prince. Petrosinella must save them both. This excellent book is currently out of print but worth seeking through inter-library loan. Alternately, check in a large reference library.

Calvino, Italo (1975). *Italian Folk Tales*. London: J. M. Dent.
This is a collection of twenty-seven stories suitable for children. It includes 'Jack and the Giant', the story of a young man who outsmarts a giant.

de Paola, Tomie (1982). *Strega Nona's Magic Lessons*. San Diego, California: Harcourt Brace Jovanovich.
This is an excellent version of the story of Strega Nona (Grandmother Witch) and her magic cooking pot which begins producing pasta at one verse, and stops when it hears another. Strega Nona's assistant remembers how to start the pot, but can't remember how to stop it, with amusing results.

Gates, Doris (1982). *The Warrior Goddess: Athena*. New York: Penguin.
A story of Athena, the daughter of Zeus, who sprang, fully-armed, from her father's forehead.

Hewitt, Kathryn (1987). *King Midas and the Golden Touch*. San Diego, California: Harcourt Brace Jovanovich.
There are many versions of this story about how a greedy king wishes that everything he touches would turn to gold. This is one of the most perceptive.

McDermott, Gerald (1980). *Sun Flight*. New York: Four Winds.
This is an excellent retelling of the story of Daedalus and Icarus, a father and son who build wings to help them escape from prison. When Icarus tries to fly to the sun, tragedy occurs because his wax-coated wings melt. This particular retelling is out of print but available in some libraries. If you can't find it, use your imagination to embellish the story of Daedalus and Icarus as told by Robert Graves in *The Greek Myths: 1* (London: Penguin, 1955).

Pyk, Ann (1972). *Hammer of Thunder*. New York: Putnam.
This is a modern retelling of a story of Zeus and his power.

MIDDLE EAST

Bushnaq, Ihea (1987). *Arab Folktales*. New York: Pantheon.
This is a translation of a number of folk tales from Arab countries.

Colum, P. (1953). *The Arabian Nights*. New York: Macmillan.
The Arabian Nights is a series of tales told by a queen to keep her husband's interest. Originally, the collection consisted of 1001 tales collected from the Middle East and India. The stories show how luck, sharp wits, a lot of money and a pretty face can help people fulfil their daydreams. Although this particular version of the stories is currently out of print, it is available in some libraries. Alternatively, use another version such as *Arabian Nights Entertainments* by Andrew Lang (New York: Dover, 1969).

Lang, Andrew (1983). *Aladdin*. New York: Penguin.
This is an excellent retelling of the story of the son of a poor Chinese tailor who outwits a Moroccan wizard to get a magic lamp. The way the boy's life is changed will intrigue young listeners.

Mehdevi, A. (1975). *Persian Folk and Fairy Tales*. New York: Knopf.
Unlike those of many other nations, Persian folk tales include a lot of irony; they also have saucy and flirtatious women. The genre includes 'pourquoi' tales such as the story of the jackal without a tail, and even a version of the three sillies. This volume is out of print but available at some libraries. If you're working with students from the Middle East, and want to include tales from their culture, ask your librarian if it is available through inter-library loan.

NORTH AMERICA

Aardema, Verna (1979). *The Riddle of the Drum*. New York: Four Winds Press.
This is a traditional tale from Tizapan, Mexico, as translated and retold by the author. Again, the book is out of print but available from some libraries. For those interested in North American myths, it is well worth the search.

Baker, B. (1973). *At the Center of the World*. New York: Macmillan.
This book outlines the creation myths of the Pima and Papago tribes of southern Arizona and northern Mexico. It is out of print but can be ordered from some university libraries.

Barbeau, Marius (1980). *The Golden Phoenix, and Other Fairy Tales From Quebec*. Don Mills, Ontario: Oxford.
When a silver apple is stolen from the king's garden, Petit Jean

follows a trail of feathers to the Glass Mountain. He goes through the mountain to find a lot of adventures and win both the Golden Phoenix and a princess's hand. This selection of French Canadian traditional tales shows the effects of the Canadian environment on European themes. 'The Princess of Tomboso' is among the eight charming tales presented by a master folklorist.

Clifton, Lucillena (1979). *The Lucky Stone*. New York: Delacorte.
A family's tradition of storytelling is highlighted as a young black girl hears her great grandmother's stories about a cherished lucky stone.

Goble, Paul (1983). *Star Boy*. New York: Bradbury Press.
This is a retelling of a Siksika legend from one of the Indian tribes of North America.

Grinnell, George Bird (1981). *The Whistling Skeleton: American Indian Tales of the Supernatural*. Edited by John Bierhorst. New York: Macmillan.
Each nationality has its own way of telling stories. So does each tribe of North American natives. This is a collection of stories about the supernatural as told by the tribes of the Great Plains.

Harris, Christie (1979). *Mouse-Woman and the Muddleheads*. New York: Atheneum.
Mouse-woman is one of the smallest legendary creatures of the northwest coast. In this Kwakiutl legend, she is also a stickler for behavior. The book is out of print but available from some of the larger libraries. Check with a university that offers courses in Native Studies.

_____ (1978). *Once More Upon A Totem*. Toronto: McClelland & Stewart.
A gifted storyteller chronicles three brief traditional tales told by the northwest Coast Indians during special gatherings and potlatches.

_____ (1984). *The Trouble With Princesses*. Toronto: McClelland & Stewart.
In these seven Tlinglit, Haida and Kwakiutl myths, the imagination of the natives of the northwest coast can be compared with that of the creators of stories about Old World princesses. In one, for example, suitors must use their wits to win Elk

Maiden. Unfortunately like many folk tale volumes, this book is now out of print. Look for it in any library that advertises a good collection of feminist literature. Alternately, check with schools offering Native Studies programs.

Hooks, William H. (1987). *Moss Gown*. New York: Ticknor & Fields.
The Old South is the setting for this American version of 'Cinderella'. The elements of rejection and triumph are included in this contemporary parallel of one of the world's most famous fairy tales.

Houston, J. (1973). *Kiviok's Magic Journey: An Eskimo Legend*. New York: Atheneum.
When raven steals the feathers from a snow goose, an eskimo must go beneath the frozen sea to find his wife and children. This tale is an excellent example of how storytellers incorporate local scenery into universal archetypes. Unfortunately the book is out of print, but still available in some collections. Ask for it in a large reference library, particularly one that specialises in North American or Inuit folklore.

Kellogg, Steven (1984). *Paul Bunyan*. New York: Morrow.
The exaggerated exploits of the legendary woodsman are retold in this energetic version of the mythical hero so popular with American audiences.

Macmillan, Cyrus (1974). *Canadian Wonder Tales*. Toronto: Clarke Irwin.
This collection outlines some of the traditional stories of the Micmac tribe of eastern Canada, and the animal fables typical of the Prairie and Pacific Coast tribes. Some show a European influence. As with so many volumes of Canadian folk tales, this book is out of print but available from some libraries. Look for it in a library that specializes in Canadiana.

Martin, Eva (1984). *Canadian Fairy Tales*. Toronto: Groundwood/Douglas & McIntyre.
A mature collection of twelve Canadian fairy tales has been gathered from the folklore of English and French settlers. A twist on the traditional 'Beauty and the Beast' story has the heroine changing from an animal to a princess.

Robinson, G. (1981). *Raven the Trickster: Legends of the North American Indian*. Toronto: Clarke Irwin.

These nine stories from the Pacific Coast tell of Raven, who likes to get the better of others and often gets himself into trouble as a result. The volume is out of print but available from some libraries, especially those that have collections of traditional native tales.

Sanders, Scott R. (1985). *Hear The Wind Blow*. New York: Bradbury Press.

Early American folk songs are retold for young listeners in this charming picture book.

Siberell, Anne (1982). *Whale in the Sky*. New York: Dutton.

This is a traditional legend of the native Indians who inhabited the northwest coast of North America.

Toye, William (1978). *How Summer Came to Canada*. Don Mills, Ontario: Oxford.

The retelling of this Micmac legend is freely based on *Canadian Wonder Tales* by Cyrus Macmillan.

RUSSIA

Bloch, M. (1974). *Ukrainian Folk Tales*. New York: Putnam.

In these twelve stories, animals mirror human foibles. One of the most interesting is the story of Seerko, an old dog who is thrown out by his master. A wolf helps him regain his home; Seerko later returns the favor. This book is out of print but available in collections such as that held in the Toronto Public Library's Boys' and Girls' House.

Chandler, R. (1980). *Russian Folk Tales*. New York: Random House.

This is a series of Russian folk tales told by Aleksander Nikolaevich Afanasev and translated by Chandler. Although the volume is out of print, check for it in a good reference library.

Cohen, M. (1980). *Lovely Vasilisa*. New York: Atheneum.

In this Russian story, a doll left by her dead mother protects a young girl—a twist on the Cinderella story that will enchant youngsters interested in the many guises Cinderella wears. Check with the largest children's collection near you, especially one that carries a lot of folk tales.

Cole, Joanna (1983). *Bony-Legs*. New York: Macmillan.
This traditional Russian tale will amuse young listeners.

Hodges, Margaret (1987). *The Little Humpbacked Horse*. New York: Farrar, Straus, & Giroux.
When a peasant's son catches the beautiful mare that is stealing the family's hay, she gives him three foals. The smallest, a little humpbacked horse, helps his master through troubles and assists him in winning a Tsaritsa.

Ginsburg, M. (1979). *The Twelve Clever Brothers*. Philadelphia: Lippincott.
This is the retelling of a popular Russian folk tale in which the number of brothers changes according to the source. It recounts how a father sends his sons on a journey to help them understand more and learn more. Their travels help the brothers become rich in observation and wisdom. The story encourages children to predict and so, although the book is out of print, it is well worth looking for in a good library.

Marshak, Samuel (1983). *The Month Brothers: A Slavic Tale*. New York: William Morrow.
This is a traditional tale about two brothers who seek wives, and about what happens when they do.

Onassis, J., ed. (1978). *The Firebird and Other Russian Tales*. New York: Viking.
Originally from Czechoslovakia, 'The Firebird' is an interesting version of the popular story about a clever younger son winning what his older brothers cannot.

Silverman, Maida (1984). *Anna and the Seven Swans*. New York: William Morrow.
This story is based on a Baba Yaga tale as retold from the Russian by Natasha Frumin. It recounts how a young girl's loyalty frees her brothers from a cruel enchantment. This excellent retelling of the popular tale is out of print but available from some libraries. If you can't find it, work with 'The Six Swans', an old German tale from the Andrew Lang collection. This tale is retold in many anthologies, including *The World's Best Fairy Tales* (New York: Reader's Digest, 1967).

Tolstoy, A. (1969). *The Great Big Enormous Turnip*. New York: Watts.

One day a man grew a turnip so big that he couldn't pull it up. This amusing pattern story will delight young listeners. Unfortunately, this particular retelling is out of print, but there are many other versions. Look for it in a good library, or use another retelling of the same tale.

SCANDINAVIA

Andersen, Hans Christian (1978). *Hans Andersen: His Classic Fairy Tales*. Translated by E. Haugaard. New York: Doubleday.
Although there are many translations of these popular Danish tales, this book includes eighteen favorites. Among them are 'The Emperor's New Clothes' and 'The Little Mermaid'.

_____ (1982). *The Snow Queen*. Retold by A. Ehrlich. New York: Dial.
When the boy Kai gets a speck of an enchanted mirror in his eye, he sees good things as bad and vice versa. As a result, he goes to live with the cruel Snow Queen until he is rescued by a loyal friend.

Asbjornsen, P. and J. Moe (1989). *East of the Sun and West of the Moon*. Retold by Kathleen and Michael Hague. San Diego, California: Harcourt Brace Jovanovich.
This Norwegian tale is about a farmer's daughter who refuses all of her suitors. When her father's fortunes later fail, she is sent on a long journey.

_____ (1961). *Favorite Fairy Tales Told In Norway*. Boston: Little, Brown.
Although currently out of print, this volume can be found in some reference libraries. It contains an interesting version of 'The Lad and the North Wind', the tale of a young boy from whom the North Wind steals a meal. Surprising things happen to the boy when he tries to get repaid for his lost dinner!

_____ (1982). *Norwegian Folk Tales*. New York: Pantheon.
In this volume, pay special attention to the 'Cinderlad' stories. Cinderlad is a youngest son who uses wit to win a princess.

Booss, Claire, ed. (1984). *Scandinavian Folk and Fairy Tales*. New York: Outlet Book Co.
This is a collection of Scandinavian tales that will interest many storytellers and their audiences.

de Gerez, T. (1986). *Louhi, Witch of North Farm: A Finnish Tale*. New York: Penguin Viking.

When Louhi locks the sun and moon away, Seppo (the heavenly blacksmith) and Vainamoinen (the Great Knower) discuss what they will do in return. Louhi is so afraid of the possible consequences of her action that she returns the sun and moon to their rightful places.

Galdone, Paul (1981). *The Three Billy Goats Gruff*. New York: Ticknor & Fields.

Across the bridge from the pasture of the three billy goats gruff is a far better pasture. Unfortunately, under the bridge lives a goat-eating troll. This Norwegian story explains how the goats outwit the troll.

Roll-Hansen, J. (1983). *A Time For Trolls*. Oslo: Tanum-Norli.

This excellent book is rare but still available in some libraries. Because of a recent interest in gnomes it is also in many private collections and, because of its unique Scandinavian flavor, is well worth the search.

SOUTH AMERICA

Bierhorst, John (1986). *The Monkey's Haircut: and Other Stories Told by the Maya*. New York: Morrow.

'The Monkey's Haircut' is about a monkey who forgets to keep the clippings when he gets his hair cut. When the hair is lost he takes the barber's razor, which he later loans to a butcher who breaks it, and must pay with a guitar. But the guitar gets the monkey into trouble. These twenty-two stories include myths, just-so stories, witch stories, and tales of animal tricksters. Some date back a thousand years; others have been borrowed from European and Asian sources.

Dewey, A. (1981). *The Thunder God's Son*. New York: Greenwillow.

Acuri is sent to earth to learn the ways of man. He learns to punish and reward in this Peruvian tale that emphasizes the importance of sharing. Because of its colorful artwork and unique language this book, which is out of print, is still part of many collections of traditional children's literature. Check with the largest children's library near you.

Jagendorf, M. (1970). *The King of the Mountains: A Treasury of Latin American Folk Stories*. New York: Vanguard.

This out of print volume includes sixty-five tales from South America and the Caribbean countries. It includes the story of the contest between the condor, eagle and hawk to see which could fly the highest. Because the condor won, the King of Heaven always takes that form when he comes to earth. For another recounting of this same tale, see *King of the Birds* by Shirley Climo.

SOUTH PACIFIC

Berndt, C. (1983). *Land of the Rainbow Snake*. Sydney: Collins.

The rainbow serpent created Australia's geological features as it slithered around the continent. It then swallowed the Bil-bil boys who begged it to protect them from a storm. What happens when humans come to rescue the Bil-bil boys explains why there are so many different kinds of animals in Australia.

Kanawa, Kiri Te (1989). *Land of the Long White Cloud: Maori Myths, Tales and Legends*. London: Pavilion Books.

Fifteen of her ancestral tribe's most exciting myths and legends are retold by Dame Kiri Te Kanawa. The story of the demi-god Maui who fished New Zealand up from the sea is one of the several 'pourquoi' tales.

Parker, K. (1976). *Australian Legendary Tales*. New York: Viking.

Originally published in 1896, this book contains fifty aboriginal stories which provide a vivacious picture of Australia as it was in the beginning. One outlines the story of a little duck who was captured by a vicious rat. Their mating resulted in the platypus.

Roughsey, Dick (1989). *The Rainbow Serpent*. Milwaukee: Gareth Stevens.

An aboriginal myth tells of Goorialla, the great Rainbow Serpent, who embarks on a quest to find his own tribe. The 'pourquoi' element of the narrative makes it ideal for a storytelling session.

Williams, J. (1979). *The Surprising Things Maui Did*. New York: Four Winds.

This Maori story outlines some of the mischief done by the half-god Maui. Because of its exceptional New Zealand flavor, it is well worth searching for in libraries that continue to carry books which are currently out of print.

UNITED KINGDOM AND IRELAND

Bishop, Gavin (1984). *Chicken Licken*. Oxford: Oxford.
This is a delightful retelling of the traditional English tale about the chicken who thinks the sky is falling when an acorn lands on her head. The fox is glad to take advantage of such ignorance.

Cauley, Lorinda B. (1982). *The Cock, the Mouse, and the Little Red Hen*. New York: Putnam.
Originally from England, this is a retelling of the story of a hard-working red hen who lives with two lazy house guests, and how a visit from a fox changes their lives.

_____ (1983). *Jack and the Beanstalk*. New York: Putnam.
This is an excellent retelling of the traditional British tale about the poor boy who trades the family cow for a handful of magic beans.

Colum, Padraic (1986). *The King of Ireland's Son*. Edinburgh: Floris Books.
This volume includes seven Irish stories in which the King of Ireland's son plays an important role.

Cooney, Barbara (1958). *Chanticleer and the Fox*. New York: Harper & Row.
Adapted from Chaucer's *Canterbury Tales*, the story contains an imaginative description of a proud rooster named Chanticleer who encounters a crafty fox.

Cooper, Susan (1983). *The Silver Cow: A Welsh Tale*. New York: Macmillan.
This is a sensitive retelling of the Welsh story about a young farm boy who receives a silver cow as a thank you for his beautiful music. When the boy's father misuses the cow, however, the family loses her and all of the fortune she has brought.

de la Mare, W. (1983). *Mollie Whuppie*. New York: Farrar, Straus and Giroux.
Three woodcutter's daughters who are lost in the woods find the home of a giant. Through craft, Mollie Whuppie, the youngest, saves both herself and her sisters. This excellent retelling

of this traditional English story is out of print but available at some libraries.

de Paola, Tomie (1981). *Fin M'Coul: The Giant of Knockmany Hill.* New York: Holiday.
De Paola tells this traditional Irish folk tale in his usual enthusiastic style.

Galdone, Paul (1981). *The Three Sillies.* Boston: Houghton Mifflin.
When a girl and her parents cry at what might happen if an ax isn't removed from the beam in their basement, the girl's boyfriend refuses to marry her until he can find three equally silly people. This traditional English tale recounts what the suitor finds.

_____ (1982). *What's In Fox's Sack?* Boston: Houghton Mifflin.
Fox puts a bumblebee in his sack, then tricks a number of people into giving him something better than he already has. In the end, however, he is outwitted. The cumulative narrative of this tale encourages children to make predictions.

Garner, Alan ed. (1984). *Book of British Fairy Tales.* London: Collins.
The author's selection of fairy tales is filled with the element of magic intended to serve as a weapon against evil. The stories are varied in mood, the style is distinguished, and the narratives read or tell beautifully.

Glassie, H. ed. (1987). *Irish Folk Tales.* London: Penguin.
This is a selection of Irish folk tales and legends edited by an eminent folklorist.

Godden, Rumer (1964). *The Dragon of Og.* London: Magnet Books.
This is the Scottish tale of a very interesting dragon.

Jones, Gwyn ed. (1979). *Welsh Legends and Folktales.* London: Penguin.
This volume relates the stories of the British King Arthur and of Branwen.

Leodhas, Sorche Nic (1978). *Sea-Spell and Moor-Magic: Tales of the Western Isles.* New York: Holt, Rinehart.
Many traditional Scottish tales include references to the sea

and the moors, aspects of Scottish life which carry their own mystery.

Montgomerie, W. and N. Montgomerie (1985). *The Well At World's End: Folk Tales of Scotland*. Edinburgh: Canongate Publishing.
This volume, which includes a bibliography and indexes, outlines some British tales useful to the storyteller.

Pyle, Howard (1903). *The Story of King Arthur and His Knights*. New York: Scribner.

This is an interesting version of this traditional story of the famous King Arthur and his Knights of the Round Table.

_____ (1968). *The Merry Adventures of Robin Hood*. New York: Dover.
This is a retelling of the traditional tale about how a nobleman hides in Sherwood Forest, where he steals from the rich to give to the poor. Encourage students to compare the original characters to those in the modern movie version. How are they the same? How and why are they different?